WAGADU VOLUME 5

WAGADU VOLUME 5

ANTI-TRAFFICKING, HUMAN RIGHTS, AND SOCIAL JUSTICE

TIANTIAN ZHENG

To order additional copies of this book, contact:
Xlibris Corporation
1-888-795-4274
www.Xlibris.com
Orders@Xlibris.com
50004

Wagadu Volume 5: Anti-Trafficking, Human Rights, and Social Justice
Guest Editor Tiantian Zheng, SUNY Cortland.
© 2009 Wagadu: A Journal of Transnational Women's and Gender Studies
State University College at Cortland,
PO Box 2000, Cortland, NY, 13045
www.wagadu.org
Mechthild Nagel, SUNY Cortland, Editor-in-Chief
Tiantian Zheng, SUNY Cortland, Managing Editor
Kathryn Coffey, SUNY Cortland, Book Review Editor
Jean Young, Cornell, New Media Review Editor
Andrew Fitz-Gibbon, SUNY Cortland, Webmaster and Publishing Advisor

Angaluki Muaka

John Mugane

Ghislaine Lydon

Nkiru Nzegwu

Kathryn Russell

Tonia St. Germain

Maina Chalwa Singh

Elizabeth Kim Stone

Jennifer Tappan

Larissa Titarenko

Brett Troyan

Philip Walsh

Betty Wambui

CONTENTS

Preface

Mechthild Nagel, Editor-in-Chief of Wagadu: A Journal of Transnational
Women's and Gender Studies
with Kassim Kone, Editor, Wagadu

With this volume, *Wagadu: A Journal of Transnational Women's and Gender Studies*
launches its third paperback edition, after publishing Volume 3 on "Water and Women in
Past, Present and Future," and Volume 4 "Intersecting Gender and Disability Perspectives
in Rethinking Postcolonial Identities" with Xlibris in 2007 and 2008. All volumes,
including Vol. 1 and 2 on critiques of imperialism and women in a global environment,
can be found free of charge at http://wagadu.org. The journal is supported by the dedicated
faculty and staff of the State University of New York, College at Cortland, USA. We thank
the office of the provost of SUNY Cortland for funding of this book. We continue to
receive support from a diverse and international advisory and editorial board membership,
making Wagadu one of the few notable postcolonial and feminist journals (online or in
print). The next volume to appear in 2008 is co-edited by Colleen Kattau and Kathryn
Russell of SUNY Cortland on the theme: "Women's Activism for Gender Equity in
Africa and the Diaspora." Kattau and Russell collaborated with editors from the Journal
of International Women's Studies to produce a joint special issue that will be released
on Wagadu and JIWS's websites.

Wagadu: What's in a Name

Wagadu—the Soninke name of the Ghana Empire—controlled the present-day Mali,
Mauritania and Senegal and was famous for its prosperity and power from approximately
300-1076. It constituted the bridge between North Africa, the Mediterranean and Middle
Eastern worlds and Subsaharan Africa. Ghana gave birth to the two most powerful West
African Empires: Mali and Songhay. The modern country of Ghana (former British Gold
Coast) derives its name from the Ghana Empire.

Legend says that Ghana's power derived from a mythic python, which generated the
rich gold deposits and controlled the fortunes of the empire. Year after year the people
of Ghana had to offer the most beautiful virgin to the python as a sacrifice. One year, the
distressed fiancé of a sacrificial girl took a sword and beheaded the mythic python in a
preemptive move. The head flew and crashed into the parts of West Africa that became

9

gold producing regions leading to the rise of the Mali Empire. Ghana fell after seven years of drought and poverty forced the Ghana people, the Soninke, to disperse and adopt exodus as a way of life to this day.

Why Wagadu? Wagadu has come to be the symbol of the sacrifice women continue to make for a better world. Wagadu has become the metaphor for the role of women in the family, community, country, and planet. The excerpt below from a Soninke song best summarizes this state of fact:

> *Duna taka siro no yagare npale*
> *The world does not go without women.*

We hope you will find this volume engaging as the authors grapple with the intersecting discourses on anti-trafficking, human rights, and social justice, edited by Tiantian Zheng, associate professor of anthropology at SUNY Cortland.

Cortland, October 2008

Editorial

Tiantian Zheng

This particular issue of Wagadu, *Journal of Transnational Women's and Gender Studies* aims to explore the life experiences, agency, and human rights of women, who are involved in a variety of activities that are characterized as "trafficked" terrains in a de-territorialized and re-territorialized world, in order to shed light on the complicated processes in which anti-trafficking, human rights and social justice are intersected. While previous studies have highlighted popular discourses, national and international policies, and the victimization and struggles of the trafficked women, few studies have centered on the stories of the migrant subjects themselves. The intent of these articles is to offer a critical reading of the recent competing definitions of trafficking and the complex ways in which the intertwined configurations of gender, race, ethnicity, and nationality complicate the contemporary hegemonic discourse on trafficking. This special issue fills this lacuna through theorizing and conceptualizing the intersecting discourses on anti-trafficking, human rights, and social justice from the perspectives of the transnational migrant populations. This issue specifically includes articles that rearticulate the trafficking discourses away from the state control of immigration and the global policing of borders, and reassert the social justice and the needs, agency, and human rights of migrant and working communities.

The articles collected in this edition cover a wide array of topics. The authors critically analyze not only the conflation of trafficking with sex work in international and national discourses and its effects on migrant women, but also the global anti-trafficking policy and the root causes for the undocumented migration and employment. In these articles, the authors address the debate between the recognition of women's human rights to migrate and work as sex workers and the anti-trafficking policy that classifies sex workers as trafficked victims and slaves. In the process, they stress the effects on the vulnerable population as a result of the anti-prostitution policy and a denial of human rights of sex workers and the socio-cultural effects on the migrant population as a result of the global and national laws against trafficking, immigration, and smuggling. The authors pinpoint the relationships between the human rights of the vulnerable population and the state approaches to trafficking. They also examine the effects upon the migrant population as a result of the ways in which the state and international policies define "trafficked persons" and "undocumented migrants," and the complicated intersections of forced and voluntary labor and migrations at the national and international level. The authors in this edition suggest more effective anti-trafficking interventions, which will ameliorate social justice and human rights of the migrant populations.

In her article, Jennifer Musto argues that the anti-trafficking movement will not be successful unless we include the voices of the trafficked people, and the government changes its position on trafficking. Musto contends that the U.S. government's position on trafficking directly influences the organization and leading ideology of NGOs. She explores how such policies have contributed to the asymmetrical power relations between NGO staff and the clients, and restrained the efficacy of the anti-trafficking movement.

Musto points out that because NGOs depend upon federal funding, organizations that accept sex work as a legitimate profession or argue against the conflation of voluntary prostitution with trafficking potentially run the risk of losing their funding. To ensure funding, NGOs must align their internal policies with the views of the U.S. government by claiming that all forms of prostitution are exploitative, equivalent of "sexual slavery," and are a "gateway" to trafficking. Musto contends that such a biased and narrow definition of trafficking influences their identification practices, as they provide shelters to the involuntary trafficked persons and arrest the voluntary migrants.

Through investigating the history, organizational structure, and program offerings of a local NGO in Los Angeles, Musto argues that the organization fails to include trafficked persons' participation in the anti-trafficking movement. Since NGOs cannot use the U.S. government funds to promote or advocate the legalization or regulation of prostitution as a legitimate form of work, it prevents the staff from having any dialogues or developing any programs with clients who have worked voluntarily in the sex industries. Within this funding culture of fear, the staff feels obligated to exclude clients who may voluntarily choose sex work for survival.

Musto further observes that there is a power hierarchy between the staff and the clients, as the staff has greater access to power and decision making, whereas the clients—the trafficked persons—are compelled to participate in programs where they are allowed little, if any, input. She concludes that the current funding pressures and power structure in NGOs have seriously curtailed the participation of trafficked persons in the anti-trafficking movement. She advocates that we should include the trafficked persons in the anti-trafficking movement, and rethink strategies and tactics that can help build upon trafficked persons' experiences and expertise.

Sholeh Shahrokhi's article focuses on the specific social/cultural conditions in which young Iranian women and children are transported into the underground prostitution circles of the Gulf-states. Her paper aims to draw scholarly attention to the cultural context surrounding sex trafficking in Iran.

Shahrokhi points out that despite the substantial role of poverty in the formation of sex-commerce and human-trafficking, the complexities of historical cultural values, attitudes, and practices towards sex deserve serious consideration. She explores how the history of polygamous practices, social construction of the Harem, and the sexual slave-markets in Iran have contributed to the formation of sexual meanings and the current attitudes toward bartering of the body.

Shahrokhi states that while the sex traffickers in the Persian Gulf area are beginning to receive some attention from the international human rights activists, there is little attempt to improve the attitudes and life-styles of the families where the flights begin. She contends that we have to pay heed to the socio-cultural context where it becomes plausible for sex-trafficking to thrive. She argues that although economic misfortune often determines the fate of young women, gender double standards cut across social classes in Iran and the tradition of sex-slavery has endured since an antiquated era. As she observes, within Shiite Islam and the Iranian adaptation of the faith, the institutionalism of temporary marriages or sigheh has legitimized marketing and bartering of the body. Prior to marriage and especially among crowded families, daughters assume their domestic role in cooking and caring for the family at a very young age.

Shahrokhi asserts that new trends of sex-trade in the Gulf region have emerged out of an accelerating poor economy for a majority of people in Iran, impoverished living situations, and a failure to educate the public about the value and rights of women. In addition, mass-migrations caused by a constellation of political revolutions and war, resurgence of religious fundamentalism, and the return of traditional cultural values towards gender provide a new niche for sex-trade to go underground and for new money to be poured into its industry.

Shahrokhi concludes that, to confront the growth of sex-trade, we have to increase our awareness and possible collaborations with the powerful industry that responds to this market, and, at the same time, contest the local traditions and sexually violent views of women that persist in the region as a breeding ground for human trafficking and underground sex trade endeavors.

Sine Plambech's article is based upon the ethnographic fieldwork conducted with a group of Thai women and Danish men in northwest rural Denmark. By placing these women's own perspectives at the centre of the analysis, Plambech's article seeks to debunk the victim-script of the mail order bride discourse on transnational marriages between Thai women and European men.

Plambech uses the ethnographic accounts to critique the existing discourse that categorizes mail order brides as victims of illegal trafficking and violence. While the anti-trafficking organizations often cite mail order brides as a target group, Plambech points out that the Thai brides are neither commodities nor victims. Their individual motives for transnational marriage include freedom from harsh working conditions, freedom from Thai gender roles, and their preconceived ideas about Danish men. According to Plambech, these women, are far from victims, and are independent and resourceful. As she demonstrates, instead of being trafficked into Denmark, the Thai women met their husbands via local women and men who were already married to a Danish husband or Thai woman, and they communicated prior to meeting through letters.

Plambech observes that anti-trafficking organizations do not distinguish between groups of migrant women, prostitutes, sex slaves, housekeepers, and mail order brides, and lump them all together as victims of trafficking. She points out that the uncritical linking of mail order brides to trafficking ignores the women's participation in the transnational migration, their contribution to a global remittance and care economy, and the women's ability to make rational decisions.

In contrast to the existing discourse that represents the mail order brides as a vulnerable group without a social network in Denmark or ties to their country of origin, Plambech argues that the Thai women in her study have both a social network and connections with their families in Thailand. As she illustrates, through migrating and regularly remitting money to Thailand, these brides become part of "an alternative global circuit," connecting their country of origin with their country of residence.

Leah Briones' article also critiques the anti-trafficking discourse that revolves around victimisation, agency, and rights. She argues that these concepts help legitimize receiving countries' border control, rather than protecting the livelihood of migrant workers. Drawing on the experiences of Filipina domestic workers in Paris and Hong Kong, Briones uses Nussbaum's Capabilities Approach to debunk the current anti-trafficking discourse.

Briones' research on domestic workers from the Philippines in Paris and Hong Kong shows that it is the question of capability (what she is actually able to do and be) rather than rights (what she is entitled to do and be) with which these workers are most immediately concerned. She concludes that the rights-based initiatives should foreground capability as the political goal. Briones criticizes the feminists' "victim/agent" script, and argues that having rights is not necessarily conducive to practices of agency when the agent is constrained. Briones interviewed twenty-four migrant workers to study the nature of these constraints, and discovered that the workers believed that the abuse and violence in the work are "natural to making money." Briones argues that their belief arises from the structural constraints, i.e., their material conditions and survival needs of their families back home. She observes that access to livelihood resources is an important measure of the capability of their agency. Briones argues that we should not frame their situation in the anti-trafficking discourse of victim vs. agents. Protecting their human rights does not guarantee them livelihood, yet protecting their livelihood creates the opportunity to secure their human rights.

Tiantian Zheng's paper is based upon over twenty months of fieldwork between 1999 and 2002 in Dalian. Zheng discusses the adverse effect upon sex workers of China's abolitionist policy that focuses on forced prostitution and launches anti-trafficking campaigns. As she demonstrates, the state's anti-trafficking campaigns lead to a violent working environment for the karaoke bar hostesses, as the hostesses are more exposed to violence by clients, policemen, madams, government officials, and bar waiters. Zheng also provides an account of how, unlike the government's perception of forced prostitution, hostesses voluntarily choose their profession and actively seek sex work in countries such as Japan and Singapore.

In a nutshell, the authors in this journal issue have successfully employed their ethnographical research to demystify the anti-trafficking discourse, rearticulate the trafficking discourses, and reassert the social justice and the needs, agency, and human rights of migrant and working communities.

One

THE NGO-IFICATION OF THE ANTI-TRAFFICKING MOVEMENT IN THE UNITED STATES: A CASE STUDY OF THE COALITION TO ABOLISH SLAVERY AND TRAFFICKING

Jennifer Lynne Musto
University of California, Los Angeles

Introduction

The ideas for this paper have emerged over the course of the past two years, in which I have sought to combine my academic research on trafficking and sex work with participatory action research and human rights activism. The latter has brought me into contact with a spate of nongovernmental organizations (NGOs), both in the Netherlands[1] and the United States,[2] that provide advocacy and social services to sex workers and trafficked persons, most of whom are women.

Scholars who are interested in conducting research on trafficking in the United States that focuses on the perspectives of individuals who have been trafficked are inevitably required to work closely, and at times, exclusively, with social service agencies (Brennan, 2005, p. 39). As a gatekeeper between trafficked persons and researchers, social service providers create and disseminate particularized definitions and ideologies of trafficking. Far from benign, social service agencies, or what are oft-referred to as "NGOs," have led the "anti-trafficking movement" in the United States by advising policymakers, training law enforcement, and drafting anti-trafficking legislation, in addition to providing a wide range of services to individuals who have been trafficked. Yet despite innumerable reports, scholarly papers, conferences, and media coverage dedicated to the subject of human trafficking, the voices of trafficked women, men, and children are seldom, if ever, heard. Doezema observes that in the absence, or what might be the strategic exclusion of trafficked persons' voices; an image of a trafficked person emerges; one that is innocent, naïve, and unable to exercise agency over his or her life. "The picture of the 'duped innocent' is a pervasive and tenacious cultural myth. High profile campaigns by NGOs and in the media, with their continued focus on the victim adds more potency to the myths . . . in reports on trafficking it is often stressed that the women did not choose to be prostitutes" (Doezema, 1998, p. 45).

It is important to note that not all sex workers are trafficked, nor are all trafficked persons forcibly and coercively moved between and within borders for the purposes of commercial sexual exploitation. Although feminists have been at the fore of discussions surrounding sex work and trafficking, not all NGOs that work with trafficked persons identify as feminists, or work from a perspective in which survivors are at the center of their social service and advocacy efforts. Indeed, NGOs whose work addresses human trafficking identify with one or more theoretical perspectives that range from abolitionist and neoabolitionist perspectives[3] to those that view trafficking on a continuum of migration,[4] as a human rights issue,[5] within a pro-sex work/labor framework,[6] and as an extension of religious/faith-based beliefs (Soderlund, 2005, p.70).

Through NGOs pro-offer valuable services to trafficked persons, this paper will explore how increased professionalization, or what may be more aptly deemed the "NGO-ification" of the anti-trafficking movement in the U.S. has curtailed trafficked persons efforts to organize a movement that speaks to their experiences and needs. In her article, "Methodological Challenges in Research with Trafficked Persons: Tales from the Field," Denise Brennan notes that "the sustainability of an anti-trafficking movement in the U.S. hinges not only on ex-captives telling their own stories, but also on taking their own active leadership role in its direction, agenda-setting, and policy making" (2005, p. 38). While I embrace Brennan's contention that a vibrant anti-trafficking movement must include the voices of trafficked persons, I argue that within the current anti-trafficking milieu in which NGOs remain overwhelmingly if not exclusively dependent on federal funding, an emergent anti-trafficking movement lead by trafficked persons seems highly unlikely if not altogether impossible.

In order to highlight the limitations of the current anti-trafficking movement as it emerged vis-à-vis U.S. NGOs, I will provide an overview of U.S. government's position on trafficking in an effort to chart how explicit policies on trafficking and the implicit ideologies they evoke influence NGOs' relationship to the federal government. From there I will explore how such policies contribute to the professionalization of the anti-trafficking movement that has contributed to asymmetrical power relations between NGO staff and the clients they "serve," while restraining an anti-trafficking movement in the United States led by those who have firsthand experience in the process of irregular movement and exploitation.

Ideological Blind Spots

Against the backdrop of highly contested international debates over how to define trafficking[7] and what, if any, linkages exist between prostitution and trafficking,[8] NGOs are given little choice but to "take sides" in discerning where they stand. For U.S. and international NGOs receiving U.S. government funding, however, divergent views on this issue have, at least publicly, been stifled following a December 2002 National Security Presidential Directive. The directive charges that, "as a result of the prostitution-trafficking link, the U.S. government concludes that no U.S. grant funds should be awarded to foreign non-governmental organizations that support legal state-regulated prostitution" (United States Department of State, 2004). Though specific to foreign NGOs, the Gag Rule extends to domestic agencies and is based on claims that trafficking thrives in areas where prostitution has been legalized and/or decriminalized.[9] As such, organizations that promote and/or accept sex work as a legitimate profession and argue against the conflation of voluntary prostitution with trafficking run the risk of losing their funding.[10] By suggesting that all forms of prostitution are exploitative, akin to "sexual slavery,"[11] and a "gateway"[12] to trafficking, NGOs that receive U.S. government funding are bound to narrow interpretations and definitions of trafficking, and, as a result, typically interface with only those trafficked persons who fit proscriptive profiles.

Anderson and O'Connell Davidson find that governmental and intergovernmental organizations are keen to position trafficking within a framework of crime control and prevention. From this vantage point, harms inflicted upon "legitimate" trafficked persons, juxtaposed to those who are deemed "voluntary" economic migrants, concurrently represent a threat to the state. "The beauty of trafficking, constructed as a problem of organized transnational crime, is that it apparently represents a form of forced migration that simultaneously involves the violation of the human rights of the 'trafficked' person and a threat to national sovereignty and security" (Anderson and O'Connell Davidson, 2002). As a result, only those individuals whose situations align with current scholarship, policy, law enforcement and NGO conceptualizations of what trafficking is and who trafficked people are, will be identified as trafficked juxtaposed to labeled as voluntary migrants.[13]

To this point, Tyldum and Brunovskis observe that "the ratio of cases identified by law enforcement or nongovernmental organizations to the total number of trafficking cases in an area is seldom known, it is difficult to determine to what extent the identified cases are representative of the universe of trafficking cases, and which biases they introduce" (2005, p. 24). Tyldum and Brunovskis's observations are noteworthy in that they draw attention to personal and institutional biases that may in practice perpetuate tendentious assessments of the "trafficking universe." What else might explain the vast discrepancy that exists between the estimated numbers of people trafficked into the United States each year and the actual number of individuals that are identified and certified[14] as victims of trafficking? Though improved methods of detection are touted as the main reason the numbers have "gone from 45,000 to 50,000 in 1999, to 18,000 to 20,000 victims reported in 2003 to 14,500 to 17,500 quoted in the 2004 TIP report," ideological biases against immigrants in general, and prostituting immigrants in particular, also appear to attribute to difficulties in identifying trafficked persons[15] (Gozdziak and Collett, 2005, p. 10). In the absence of research that systematically assesses the extent to which law enforcement and NGO biases influence identification practices, it seems reasonable to assume that NGOs, like the governments that fund them, perpetuate ideological blind spots in negotiating a trafficking terrain where moralizing discourse stands in for conclusive empirical data.[16]

Awkward Alliances: Brief Contextualization of the Division of Labor Between the U.S. Government and NGOs

Aside from the ways in which selective seeing delimits understanding about trafficking, what seems additionally perplexing is the degree to which NGOs are capable of maintaining critical distance from government policies. William Fisher notes that although "NGOs are purely voluntary groups with no governmental affiliation or support, some groups so designated are created and maintained by governments . . . while the moniker 'nongovernmental organization' assumes autonomy from governments, NGOs are often intimately connected with their governments" (2005, p. 451). Though an in-depth exploration of the ways in which NGOs reproduce, re-entrench, and resist governmental practices remains outside the scope of this paper, it seems important to point out the obvious: not all NGOs are "good," progressive, nor inherently invested in struggling toward social justice with the individuals for whom they work. Moreover, since NGOs in the United States increasingly function as an extension or dislocated arm of state sponsored policies, it behooves scholars, policy makers, and community stakeholders alike to critically interrogate the role that they play in ameliorating trafficking on the one hand, and whether they help, hinder, complicate, and/or facilitate trafficked persons' empowerment on the other.

As a "hot topic," that has captured the public imaginary, policy makers, researchers, and activists press for greater resources to curtail trafficking. Regardless of their ideological position regarding prostitution or immigration, a consistent thread throughout the scholarly, intergovernmental, and NGO literature is that more attention and funds are needed to assist trafficked persons (Zarembka, 2003; Bump and Duncan, 2003; Chuang, 2005). The Trafficking Victims Protection Act (TVPA) of 2000 and its Reauthorization in 2003 draw upon a three-pronged approach, or what is known as the three "P's": to prevent trafficking, prosecute traffickers, and protect trafficked persons (Bump and Duncan, 2003).

Despite its rhetorical catchiness, the U.S. government has focused more of its energies on prosecution than on prevention and protection. Chuang notes, "efforts to combat trafficking have proceeded from a narrow view of trafficking as a criminal justice problem, with a clear focus of targeting the traffickers and, to a lesser extent, protecting their victims" (2005, p. 148). As a result of the U.S. government's prioritization of prosecution over protection, by default, NGOs have been delegated the responsibility of protecting victims. Rerouting the responsibility of victim protection from the state to NGOs is evidenced by Ambassador John Miller's recent comments:

> "There is no question about it . . . carrying out the "three P's" of dealing with human trafficking—prosecution, protection and prevention—requires a great role for NGOs, protection particularly. Our policy is to reach out to local NGOs and especially get to the smaller NGOs that are on the ground doing the work" (Alta, 2006).

Though Ambassador Miller deems NGOs to be the ideal protectors of trafficked persons, the question remains as to what kind of trafficked woman, man, or child is "worthy" of protection. Furthermore, there is no evidence to confirm that the vast resources dedicated to the three P's have worked. Despite the annual availability of 5,000 T-Visas, earmarked specifically for persons trafficked into the United States, approximately 800 have been granted since the passing of the Trafficking Victims Protection Act (Hayes, 2004; Meyer, 2006). Herein, Wendy Chapkis's observations are instructive. She writes, "the Trafficking Victims Protection Act helps to define compassionate conservativism: a willingness to provide assistance and protection for a few while reinforcing barriers to help for the many. The law insists that victims deserve support because they differ from economic migrants who have unfairly benefited from facilitated migration" (2005, p. 59, emphasis mine).

Thus, in order to play the "great role" that Ambassador Miller has in mind, NGOs must align their internal policies and philosophies with the views of their funders, namely, the U.S. government. In doing so, they must implicitly distinguish between voluntary economic migrants and involuntary trafficked persons (read women trafficked for sexual exploitation) where the latter are given shelter and protection and the former are arrested and deported. Though the topic of immigration does not arouse the same kind of voyeuristic "sexiness" as sexual slavery, forced prostitution, organ removal and the like, I would wager that given the current backlash against immigration in general, and illegal "economic" immigrants living in the United States in particular, trafficking NGOs might one day face yet another Gag Rule in which only those organizations that support the "regular" movement of individuals across borders will be granted federal funding.

Although seemingly far-fetched, this example is intended to illustrate the effect that funding can have in suppressing legislative dissent. At best, the outsourcing of victim protection from the state to NGOs can provide trafficked persons with greater security and comfort, particularly since their role appears to be more ameliorative than punitive. At worst, however, this division of labor can lead to satellite state building in which only those NGOs who tow the "compassionate conservative" line are able to survive. Needless to say, dependency on governmental funding, particularly U.S. federal funding, has the potential to blunt NGOs' willingness to challenge the policies of the government that funds them (Clark, 1998).

Enter CAST

Thus far, I have endeavored to present points of interest and contention by highlighting how ideological blind spots and state-sponsored outsourcing of victim protection to NGOs creates a confusing and all too often contradictory environment for trafficked persons to navigate. I would now like to turn my attention away from overarching structural issues and refocus my energies on the Los Angeles based NGO, the Coalition to Abolish Slavery and Trafficking (CAST). By exploring their history, organizational structure, funding streams, and program offerings, I hope to gauge if CAST's "client-centered" model proves effective in encouraging trafficked persons' participation in the U.S. based anti-trafficking movement.

History and Structure

The formation of CAST came on the heels of an August 1995 immigration raid in which approximately 80 migrants from Thailand were found to be working in slave-like conditions within a compound in El Monte, California. What distinguished the El Monte situation from previous cases involving illegal immigrants working in the manufacturing, agriculture, construction, domestic service, and hotel and restaurant industries was the scope and scale of coercion involved in confining the workers in the armed compound. When the Thai workers were discovered, "75 women and 5 men had been working for 17 hours a day for seven years, sleeping eight to ten people in a room" (Taylor and Jamieson, 1999, p. 262). The case proved additionally perplexing for law enforcement and social service providers who struggled to determine their legal status. Were the Thai workers illegal immigrants and therefore subject to deportation or rather were they exploited victims entitled to visas, legal recourse, and compensation?[17] The El Monte case gave rise to an ongoing discussion amongst social service providers, law enforcement, and community leaders about how to best address the exploitation of illegal immigrants while exploring the various factors that contribute to the forced movement of people into Los Angeles County.

In an effort to attend to the specific and nuanced needs of such exploited immigrants in Los Angeles County, CAST was formed in 1998 by a small group of community activists, many of whom were directly and indirectly involved with the El Monte case. With a central mission aimed at "assisting persons trafficked for the purpose of forced labor and slavery-like practices, and to work toward ending all instances of such human rights violations" CAST offers a range of social services to trafficked persons, including providing training to law enforcement and community stakeholders, and participating in policy advocacy (Kim, 2006, p. 11). Organizationally, CAST doubles as a provider of social services on the one hand, and as a center for advocacy on the other.

As the first organization in the United States dedicated to working exclusively with survivors of trafficking, CAST was also one of the first in the U.S. to frame trafficking as a labor and human rights abuse rather than an issue implicitly related to prostitution and commercial sexual exploitation (CAST, 2007). Though the positioning of trafficking as a human rights violation juxtaposed to a form of gender based violence is perhaps related to CAST's formative experiences with the El Monte case, it has arguably proven to be one of its most strategic moves in sidestepping debates about the merits of sex work as a legitimate form of labor. Sally Engle Merry describes a successful NGO as one that "builds an issue that has a name, evokes sympathy, defines a villain, and compels a form of action. Such issues are fundamental to attracting media attention and donor support. In a sense, these issues become commodities" (2005, p. 251). Through that lens, CAST is a successful NGO par excellance; they denounce exploitative slave-like labor practices, deem traffickers to be the main culprit in perpetuating abuses, assist trafficked persons in obtaining housing, legal, health and mental health services, and draw upon their organizational capital by successfully securing U.S. government funding.

Funding

In addition to funding the vast majority of research on trafficking in the United States, (Gozdziak and Collett, 2005), the U.S. government has also been a major funder of NGOs that work with trafficked persons, particularly since the advent of the TVPA in 2000 and its corollary funding streams (Spangenberg, 2003). As a result of increased federal funding, CAST has organizationally expanded. In 2004, thanks to a $1 million grant from the Department of Justice's Office for Victims of Crime, CAST opened the first shelter for trafficked persons in the United States. It is worth noting that excluding a small amount of private donations, the overwhelming bulk of CAST operational funding comes from the Office of Victims of Crime (OVC), a federal agency within the Department of Justice, and the Office of Refugee Resettlement (ORR), which is housed within the Department of Health and Human Services (DHHS). Though difficult to precisely chart the ways in which government funding streams are translated into CAST's programs, the available data suggests that federal funding, namely funds from the OVC and ORR, is used to sponsor programs for victim support that include, but are not limited to: housing, physical and mental health care services, intensive case management, job training, and education. With additional OVC funding, CAST has developed programs to train local government, as well as Federal FBI and ICE agents, and Department of Justice employees based in Los Angeles in better identifying victims of trafficking (Kim, 2006, p. 11; U.S Department of Justice, 2006).

The infusion of funding to an organization that trains government employees and law enforcement questions the ability of CAST to retain critical distance from its funders, and to challenge current trafficking policies. To elucidate this point, the DOJ Law Enforcement Task Force and Services for Human Trafficking Victims grant, from which CAST has received funding, states in no uncertain terms that, "U.S. nongovernmental organizations cannot use U.S. government funds to lobby for, promote, or advocate the legalization or regulation of prostitution as a legitimate form of work . . . the U.S. government is opposed to prostitution and related activities, which are inherently harmful and dehumanizing" (Department of Justice, 2006).

Such staunch opposition to any form of sex work certainly delimits opportunities for dialogue and the development of programs with CAST clients who may have worked, forcibly or voluntarily, in the sex trade industries. Within such a funding culture of fear, CAST staff must buttress U.S. opposition to all forms of sex work at the expense of clients who may, of their own volition, choose sex work as a viable economic option. How, for example, might a CAST case manager respond to a client's interest in working in the sex trade, particularly if the client sees sex work as her most economically advantageous option? Though hypothetical, this example is intended to draw attention to the bind that service providers face in attempting to balance their client-centered services with funding guidelines that strictly prohibit the mere mention of sex work. Sufficient to say that CAST social service providers and advocates are in the difficult position of balancing the needs of clients with those of their funders, where the former are inextricably bound to the mainstream mores and guidelines of the latter. Equally symbolic are the ways in which such a "top-down" approach stifles trafficked persons from articulating what an anti-trafficking movement might look like to them. How do trafficked persons understand survivorship, empowerment, and social justice and how does CAST address their clients' needs through their current program offerings? In the absence of programs, and research for that matter, that bring trafficked persons into the fold of organizational decision making and program development, CAST clients are left to "survive" on the sidelines of the anti-trafficking movement.

In discussing the state's role in creating funding guidelines for domestic violence shelters, Abraham finds that, "shelters that use state resources have to work within the confines of bureaucratic structures and must therefore conform to state-defined specifications" (Abraham, 2000, p. 160). U.S. based trafficking organizations that receive federal grant money are similarly compelled to direct money towards services, campaigns, and prevention efforts that meet federally mandated guidelines. While state-defined specifications and outcomes are not unique to NGOs working with trafficked persons, specific to the issue of trafficking is the overwhelming energy dedicated to separating "deserving" trafficked victims from "undeserving" economic migrants. Such distinctions are tenuous at best, leaving NGOs like CAST with little option but to limit their services to individuals who fit prevailing definitions of who a trafficked person is and what programs staff, along with their federal funders, deem to be most efficacious in cultivating a successful survivor. So despite, or perhaps in light of, the invaluable services that CAST provides individuals who are officially identified as trafficked, funder's guidelines nevertheless prove significant in narrowing the scope in which the organization constructs the U.S. based anti-trafficking movement.

Professionalization and Programs

While the professionalization of trafficking NGOs has expanded their role in producing knowledge about trafficking, it has concurrently solidified their position as gatekeepers and "experience managers" of trafficked persons. Due to the criminal nature of trafficking and the very real safety risks that trafficked persons face once they escape their traffickers, NGO staff are called to stand-in for their clients by representing their experiences to law enforcement, DHHS, and the media. However, what remains unclear are the ways in which staff balance and synthesize the organization's interests with those of the clients they represent, and their own. Like funding constraints, a professionalized environment has the potential to exclude trafficked persons from participating in a larger anti-trafficking movement, particularly where staff are hired and paid for their professional competence and expertise in the field of trafficking, not necessarily for their activist commitments. This is not to say that CAST staff are not fully committed human right activists on their own, yet in organizationally dividing their efforts between social service and advocacy work, both of which are inextricably bound to government policies and funding outcomes, their ability to build an anti-trafficking movement inclusive to trafficked persons is markedly hindered.

Denise Brennan observes that trafficked persons have not been active in promoting anti-trafficking legislation, nor have they helped to shape the direction of the anti-trafficking movement. She further notes that, "the anti-trafficking movement is still so new in the United States that most often non-ex-captives must 'speak for' most ex-captives, if their story is to be told at this time. The movement activists, at this early stage of the fight against trafficking, are generally elites, often human rights attorneys" (Brennan, 2005, p. 43). Brennan attributes the lack of participation of trafficked persons in the anti-trafficking to the issue's relative "newness." Additional reasons have been offered to explain why survivors have not been active in speaking on their own behalf that include, "fear of reprisals from their traffickers, their [trafficked persons] stage in the recovery process, and concern that their community of co-ethnics will stigmatize them" (Brennan, 2005, p. 43).

While Brennan's points are well founded, I would add that in the context of CAST, trafficked persons are compelled to interface with staff on two conflicting levels: on the one hand, clients are "served" by staff, and on the other, they are asked to communicate with staff as dialogue partners in the anti-trafficking movement. Here it seems that in trafficked persons' roles as "client," however partial and fluid that identity may be, their ability to communicate on a level-playing field with staff is restricted, since CAST employees have greater access to power and decision making. Moreover, as clients, trafficked persons are compelled to participate in programs in which they have little, if any, input. For example, during the 2005-06, CAST entered into collaboration with the University of California, Los Angeles through the UCLA in LA program.[18] The grant aimed to connect UCLA students with CAST clients in developing art workshops and classes as creative methods of departure in rethinking the anti-trafficking movement. As a student participant in the UCLA/CAST activities, I was stunned to discover that the clients had not been asked if they wanted to participate (new shelter residents must participate in all activities), and that they had not been consulted in the planning process. My concerns came to a fore when one workshop participant poignantly asked me, "What are you doing here? What do you get out of this?" While I assumed that the project's aims were made clear to CAST clients and staff alike, the workshop participant's sharp questioning exposed a lack of communication between staff and clients, and raised doubt about clients' willingness to participate in programs, much less the organization's anti-trafficking efforts, in the absence of full disclosure and participation in decision making processes.

Since the anti-trafficking movement in the US is overwhelmingly led by a group of educated female professionals who have the ability to legally work in the United

States, questions abound as to whether such a professionalized environment is capable of creating an inclusive space in which trafficked persons can voice their needs, concerns and visions of what an anti-trafficking movement looks like based on their experiences and perspectives. Because CAST staff come from such disparate racial, gender, ethnic, educational and class backgrounds than the clients they work with, more in-depth research is needed to better understand how power and privilege operate in determining who gets to speak on behalf of trafficked persons and on what terms. Such reflections on asymmetrical power relations might also serve as an opportunity to reconceptualize what a survivor-centered environment might look like.

Despite funding pressures and professionalization, CAST has encouraged two programs that appear to foster more inclusive client participation in the anti-trafficking movement. The first, Rays of Hope, is a collection of artists based in Los Angeles who make and sell handicrafts in an effort to achieve economic independence. Rays of Hope was spearheaded by current and former CAST clients invested in gaining financial autonomy while promoting public education about trafficking. Although CAST provided the social space for Rays of Hope participants to meet one another, their activities are separate from the larger organization. While Rays of Hope participants have not, to date, articulated how their organizing efforts fit within the larger U.S. based anti-trafficking movement, and what, if any coalitions they are interested in building with trafficking NGOs, they are nevertheless one of the few survivor-centered spaces in which trafficked women and men can organize themselves independent from organizations run exclusively by non-trafficked persons. Future research might further interrogate if survivor-centered activities and organizing are more effective than professionally defined victim/client-centered models in fostering trafficked persons' healing and political mobilization.

The Survivor Advisory Caucus, which is part of CAST's Advocacy and Training Program, also appears to actively promote client participation in the organization's anti-trafficking efforts. Developed as a forum for clients to discuss their insights about trafficking policies, the Survivor Advisory Caucus has proffered clients with opportunities to express their ideas and concerns for future programs that might be meaningful to them. The Survivor Advisory Caucus remains committed to ensuring that "public policies are victim-centered," and invites client feedback on new trafficking research and legislation (CAST, 2007). The meetings are semi-structured and facilitated by the CAST Advocacy Coordinator. Clients that participate in the Survivor Advisory Caucus have also been invited to speak at law enforcement trainings and to share their stories with the media.

Without undermining the value of both Rays of Hope and the Survivor Advisory Caucus, my concern is nevertheless on the fact that these programs' participatory structure is more the exception than the rule. It remains to be seen whether CAST can extend such participatory practices to broader organizational participation, which may include hiring former clients as case managers and peer educators, involving clients in fundraising, offering organizational support for programs developed by and for clients, sponsoring law enforcement trainings and educational curricula designed by trafficked persons, and providing clients with tools that will allow them to organize their own conferences and anti-trafficking activities. Only by carving out literal and symbolic space within CAST's organizational structure and program offerings, will trafficked persons be better equipped to sustain and lead the U.S anti-trafficking movement.

Concluding Thoughts

Current funding pressures and professionalization mute, if not altogether curtail, the participation of trafficked persons in the U.S. anti-trafficking movement. CAST must negotiate a highly professionalized environment informed by policy and funder demands while advocating for trafficked persons in ways that do not further deny their agency and ability to fully participate in the anti-trafficking movement. Yet the cultivation of a survivor-centered anti-trafficking movement in the U.S. requires the willingness of NGOs to share leadership and control over anti-trafficking activities. Programs like Rays of Hope, and the Survivor Leadership Caucus demonstrate that more participatory frameworks are possible within, and outside, professionalized settings, though they require NGO professionals' concerted dedication to addressing divisions of power and privilege that exist between trafficked and non-trafficked persons. By deconstructing the ways in which governmental and organizational demands silence trafficked persons' voices, CAST can begin to rethink strategies and tactics that build upon trafficked persons' experiences and expertise, not merely in preventing trafficking in the future, but in working with individuals who have already left their trafficking situation.

References

Abraham, Margaret. (2000). *Speaking the Unspeakable: Marital Violence among South Asian Immigrants in the United States.* New Brunswick, NJ: Rutgers University Press, 2000.

Alta, Judy. (2006). Private, nonprofit groups lead fight against human trafficking. Retrieved June 10, 2006, from the United States International Information Programs Web site: http://usinfo.state.gov/xarchives/display.html

Anderson, B. and O'Connell Davidson, J. (2002). *Trafficking—A demand led problem?* Stockholm, Sweden: Save the Children Sweden.

Aronowitz, Alexis A. (2001). Smuggling and trafficking in human beings: The phenomenon, the markets that drive it and the organizations that promote it. *European Journal of Criminal Policy and Research* 9(2), 163-195.

Barry, Katheleen. (1979). *Female sexual slavery.* New York: New York University Press.

Brennan, Denise. (2005). Methodological challenges in research with trafficked persons: Tales from the field. *International Migration,* 43(1/2), 35-54.

Bump, M.N. & Duncan, J. (2003). Conference on identifying and serving child victims of trafficking. *International Migration* 41(5), 201-218.

CAST. (2007). Retrieved January 3, 2007, from http://www.castla.org

Chapkis, Wendy. (2005). Soft glove, punishing fist: The trafficking victims protection act of 2000. In Berstein, E. & Schaffner, L. (Eds.), *Regulating sex: The politics of intimacy and identity* (pp. 51-65). New York, NY: Routledge.

Clarke, G. (1998). Non-governmental organizations and politics in the developing world. *Political Studies*, 46(1), 36-52.

Chuang, Janie. (2006). Beyond a snapshot: Preventing human trafficking in the global economy. *Indiana Journal of Global Legal Studies*, 13(1), 137-163.

Fisher, William F. (1997). Doing good? The politics and antipolitics of ngo practices. *Annual Review of Anthropology*, 26, 439-464.

Gallagher, Anne. (2001). Human rights and the new UN protocols on trafficking and migrant smuggling: A preliminary analysis. *Human Rights Quarterly*, 23(4), 975-100.

Gozdziak, E.M. & Collett, E.A. (2005). Research on human trafficking in North America: A review of the literature. *International Migration*, 43(1/2), 99-128.

Haynes, Dina Francesca. (2004). Used, abused, arrested and deported: Extending immigration benefits to protect the victims of trafficking and to secure the prosecution of traffickers. *Human Rights Quarterly*, 26(2), 221-272.

Hughes, Donna. (2000). The natasha trade: Transnational sex trafficking. *National Institute of Justice*, January, 1-9.

Kelly, Liz. (2005). You can find anything you want: A critical reflection on research on trafficking in persons within and into Europe. *International Migration*, 43(1/2), 235-265.

Kempadoo, K. & Doezema, J. (Eds.). (1998). *Global sex workers: Rights, resistance and redefinition*. New York, NY: Routledge.

Kim, Gilbert. (2006). Lost children: Addressing the under-identification of trafficked alien minors in Los Angeles County. Retrieved December 15, 2006, from the UCLA Ralph and Goldy Lewis Center for Regional Policy Studies Web site: http://lewis.sppsr.ucla.edu/publications/studentreports.cfm

Kligman, G. & and Limoncelli, S. (2005). Trafficking women after socialism: To, through and from Eastern Europe." *Social Politics*, 12(1), 118-140.

Kyle, D. & Dale, J. (2001). Smuggling the state back in: Agents of human smuggling reconsidered. In Kyle, D. & and Koslowski, R. (Eds.), *Global human smuggling: Comparative perspectives* (pp. 29-57). Baltimore: John Hopkins University Press.

Laczko, Frank. (2005). Introduction: Data and research on human trafficking. *International Migration*, 43(1/2), 5-16.

Merry, Sally Engle. (2005). Anthropology and activism: Researching human rights across porous boundaries. *PoLAR: Political and Anthropology Review*, 28(2), 240-257.

Meyer, Paul. (2006, May 7). Sex slaves or capitalists? Dallas brothel raids fuel debate on human trafficking laws. *The Dallas Morning News*. Retrieved June 10, 2006, from http://www.dallasnews.com/sharedcontent/dws/news/politics/local/stories/

Naples, Nancy. (1998). *Community activism and feminist politics: Organizing across race, class, and gender*. New York, NY: Routledge.

Outshoorn, Joyce. (2005). The political debates on prostitution and trafficking of women. *Social Politics*, 12(1), 141-155.

Spangenberg, Mia. International trafficking of children to New York City for sexual purposes. Retrieved December 12, 2006, from the ECPAT-USA Web site: http://www. ecpatusa.org/reports.asp

Soderlund, Gretchen. (2005). Running from the rescuers: New U.S. crusades against sex trafficking and the rhetoric of abolition. *NWSA Journal*, 17(3), 64-87.

Sweatshop Watch. (1999, Fall). El Monte Thai garment workers: Slave sweatshops. Sweatshop Watch Newsletter 5(1). Retrieved November 11, 2006, from http://www. sweatshopwatch.org/newsletters.

Taylor I. & Jamieson, R. (1999). Sex trafficking and the mainstream of market culture. *Crime, Law, and Social Change*, 32, 257-278.

Tyldum, G. & Brunovskis, A. (2005). Describing the unobserved: Methodological challenges in empirical studies on human trafficking. *International Migration*, 43(1/2), 17-34.

United States Department of Justice. (2006). Law enforcement task forces and services for human trafficking. Retrieved November 13, 2006, from http://www.ojp.usdoj. gov/BJA/grant/06_Trafficking_Victims.pdf

United States Department of State (2004). The link between prostitution and trafficking. Retrieved June 1, 2006 from http://www.state.gov/r/pa/ei/rls/38790.htm

United States Department of State. (2006). Victims of trafficking and violence protection act of 2000: Trafficking in persons report. Retrieved July 20, 2006, from Office to Monitor and Combat Trafficking in Persons via U.S. State Department Access: http://www.state.gov/g/tip/rls/tiprpt/2006/

Zarembka, Joy M. (2003). America's dirty work: Migrant maids and modern-day slavery. In B. Ehrenreich, B. and A. Russell Hochschild, eds., *Global woman: Nannies, maids, and sex workers in the new economy* (pp. 142-153). New York, NY: Metropolitan Books.

Two

WHEN TRAGEDY HITS:
A CONCISE SOCIO-CULTURAL ANALYSIS OF SEX TRAFFICKING
OF YOUNG IRANIAN WOMEN

Sholeh Shahrokhi
University of California, Berkeley

Abstract

In this paper, I focus predominantly on the cultural context of sex trafficking of young Iranian women into the underground markets of the Persian Gulf region. Neither human trafficking nor sex trade is a modern trait. While these age-old practices have been the subject of protest by the moralists and the liberal feminists alike, the discourse of eradication of human trafficking and the restoration of the abject bodies rarely includes a remedy to revise the local and common gendered belief that allows these informal economies to proliferate.

New trends of sex-trade in the Gulf region have emerged out of a cluster of cultural and social matters, with their roots in political history of the people in the area. A few of the contributing factors that make up the social and political constellation resulting to the thriving market in human and sex trafficking are an accelerating poor economy that results in impoverished living situations for the majority of people in Iran and a failure to educate the public about the potentials and the rights of women.

Although economic misfortune often determines the fate of young women, gender double standards cut across social classes in Iran. Young girls from different regions in the country experience a variety of limitations according to local practices and hegemonic beliefs. Similarly, with respect to treatment of women by men, Iranian oral and textual history is frequently used to legitimize male dominance in contemporary life. Throughout the ages, despite warfare and social unrest, cultural continuity is preserved in the region by keeping stringent rules of conduct. Moreover, much of the popular values are learned through proverbs and legendary stories that get passed on through continuous oral reiterations. Unfortunately, included in the oral culture of the country are stories about women as being lesser to the men. The descriptive teachings of our literary past on how to train a woman into her proper obedient place is neither scarce nor trivial. In short, this article aims to pay closer attention to how a young girl comes to perceive herself and is perceived by others before she is swept up and transported into the underground sex markets abroad.

Prelude

How does one write about a problem among a people halfway around the world, when the world is sharply divided into camps of opposites where the political atmosphere is highly polarized and the military rhetoric of "belonging to one or the other" seems infinite?[1] "Imagined" or not (Anderson, 1989), national identities and community affiliations run deep in the current discourses about all that relates to life in Iran. As I write the final addendums to this article on human trafficking in Iran, I am surrounded by the language of nationalism and political significance, both in terms of the energy confrontations in the world, and at a historically significant moment when an over-achieving multi-millionaire affords to tour the outer space. Anoushe Ansari, a successful business-woman, a resident of the U.S. and a citizen of the world, unequivocally speaks of her Iranian nationality at a moment of maximum visibility in the public eye—on her travel to space. Subsequently, the possibility (or lack) of wearing the three-color Iranian flag—that powerful icon of political and national affiliation since the ancient times—becomes the topic of endless discussions. While a careful investigation of the political implications and cultural significance of Ansari's actions deserve consideration beyond the scope of this paper, I have directed my attention to a more relevant problem. Thus, how does one formulate a thoughtful script about human-trafficking practices and attitudes toward sexuality in Iran, avoiding the ambush of a language of anti-nationalism?

Questions such as these have been central in my thought process both during fieldwork in Tehran and with respect to subsequent reflection and writing. One practical approach customary to social sciences is that which relies on formulating comparisons between binary opposites—in this case between the experiences of sex-workers in Iran and its "other"—the U.S. Although the comparative methodology between the seemingly opposites in order to demystify pre-conceptions is bona fide, in order to surpass binary assessment all together, this paper offers instead a wide-ranging perspective on the topic of its inquiry. On one level, this paper considers hierarchies of social statuses and dissimilarities between different groups of Iranian female sex-workers (brought in either by force or by choice) in order to better comprehend the circumstances of their involvement in the commerce. Moreover, the study takes into account a cluster of influential socio-cultural factors that contribute to the development of the practice. Located within a complex web of norms and practices which range from the consequential effects of poverty and addiction, local perceptions of gender and sexuality, and the well-established adaptation of religious meanings, this paper reveals the transference of Iranian girls into Dubai's sex-market as a cultural construct.

The Argument

Often, the sheer catastrophic scale and details of the global underground sex markets are so extreme that to study them becomes a cumbersome ordeal, layered with political risks and emotional impediments for the researcher. While many commit to eradicating such tragic human experiences, it is crucial to note that before any fundamental changes can take root, the complexities of the socio-political context surrounding this issue need to be considered. One can study Human Trafficking from a variety of perspectives. For example, in terms of the historical development and evolution of the slave-market, criminology of sex-trade, or the socio-economic basis for human trafficking, all will provide relevant and useful analyses and findings on the topic. However, the focus of this paper is on specific social/cultural conditions, in which young Iranian women and children are transported into the underground prostitution circles of the Gulf-states. This article aims to draw scholarly attention to the cultural context surrounding sex trafficking in Iran.

The triangular movement of human trafficking between Iran, Pakistan, and UAE in recent years can be specifically divided in two separate categories and paths. Since the mid 1990's, an increasingly young population of urban females, many of whom came from an emerging class of runaway teens in the Iranian cities, have entered the Iran-UAE body-trade. This trend is also evident in the abundance of official reports, despite attempts to heighten sensitivities on the issue in the region. "In recent years, the rate of smuggling young women and the mandatory migration of the [Iranian] girls to the Gulf States and in some cases to Asian and European countries has risen sharply" (ISNA, 2004). The Tehran-Dubai path is mostly exclusive to urban runaways and young prostitutes. "Iranian girls hold the highest price and have the most appeal in smuggling markets of girls and women in the U.A.E." (Aref News, 2005).

In the year 2000, I had returned briefly to Iran after years of immigration, in order to observe life in Tehran, and to evaluate the possibility for conducting a dissertation research on teenage runaways in the city. By observing their social practices, I had hoped to understand the cultural context and political economy of a sexual morality, which teenage runaways simultaneously provoke and threaten. The conversation I overheard on my time off from fieldwork was intriguing to me, both as it related to the topic of my studies, and in the way the conversationalists boldly discussed in public a topic I had presumed taboo.

On December 2000, after recreation in the crystal waters of the coral reef in the Persian Gulf, I came ashore to the white sands of the "women-only" beaches of Kish Island. As I lay there, with my eyes closed, I overheard a conversation between two young women that perked my ears. The women were discussing a new opportunity to work in the sex-industry in Dubai. One of the women made a proposition to the younger one to take part in a classy escort service ("a service with class," in their words). Their conversation included keywords such as "a high-class setting" where "beautiful, young, Iranian girls" could meet "powerful" rich clients in Dubai-city. When the woman expressed hesitation, she was offered instead, to perform sex acts on a live internet-based web site. She was further reassured by the slightly older woman (no more than mid-twenties) that her face would not be shown, to protect her privacy. The exclusivity of both the performers and their clients, as members of a "high class" society were emphasized throughout the conversation. In one instant, the lines of distinctions were drawn to demonstrate exclusivity of this crowd from ordinary prostitutes, "street-workers," and the "runaways" (Fieldjournal, 2001:114).

It warranted no surprise to me when the reported accounts of the subsequent years suggested that women of this group enter the market with a level of awareness about sex-trade. "Majority of the Iranian girls active in the sex-commerce in the Gulf, not only are aware of their social position and their occupation, they have entered these [the Arab countries of the Gulf] for this purpose, in the first place," writes Rafiezade an Iranian journalist (IF-ID, 2005). Members of this group often see themselves as belonging to a higher and more prestigious social class in contrast to street-workers, and demonstrate a degree of "middle-class" cultural standards. These women frequently describe their status and legitimize their actions through adaptation of concepts such as "choice," "autonomy" and "personal freedom" and "financial independence."

Alternatively, human traffickers frequently use another popular route in order to smuggle women and children from Iran into the sex-markets in Dubai. This second line of movement falls in the category of more traditional smuggling operations, across multiple borders—mostly from the southern provinces adjacent to the Persian Gulf. Recently, a few cases of the abduction of children in an attempt to smuggle them abroad have been reported in papers.[2] However, because of extreme poverty, growing problems of drug addiction and overpopulation in the area, many impoverished families "marry off" their daughters, in exchange for a modest fee. In this vein, a history of patriarchy in which the value of a female is primarily restricted to her sexuality plays an important role in determining the fate of these young girls. In recent years, there has been an increase in the number of recorded incidents, where young girls were married off to an external ethnic group such as the Baluch, Pakistani, or Arab men in exchange for money. "Iran is the origin, mediation ground and a site of trafficking of numerous young women and girls for sexual exploitation." (Special Report by Farzam, 2006).

Most recently, the abolitionist movement has focused the world's attention on the criminology of human trafficking and the abuse of human rights. "Human traffickers prey on the most vulnerable and turn a commercial profit at the expense of innocent lives" (Condoleeza Rice, Secretary of State, USA, 2006). While the inhumane and criminal acts of the sex traffickers in the Persian Gulf area are beginning to receive some attention from the international human rights activists, there is little attempt to improve the attitudes and life-styles of the families where the flights begin. It is my aim to draw attention, instead, to the socio-cultural context, where it becomes plausible for sex-trafficking to thrive.

Although economic misfortune often determines the fate of young women, gender double standards cut across social classes in Iran. Girls in Iran learn about their inferiority to boys at an early age. For many families in Iran, having a female child is perceived as a burden. On the one hand, gender biases in society limit the possibilities for young

31

women to enter the work force and to engage in a stable income-generating activity, thus demoting her to an inconvenience, as an additional mouth to feed. On the other hand, unless men of kin carefully attend to her as a sexual being, girls potentially create situations that jeopardize family honor. Therefore, her guardian's priority is to teach her how to provide care to her younger siblings, to assist in the matters of domestic life to prepare her for marriage. In other words, modern conceptions of choice, compatibility of the matrimonial pair, and romance are rarely a factor in determining her fate. In most instances, harsh living conditions and economic pressures often result in disposition of the young girls, who are married off quickly, often to considerably older men, in order to avoid social embarrassment and financial hardship.

In this regard, despite the substantial role of poverty in the formation of sex-commerce and human-trafficking, the complexities of cultural values, attitudes, and practices towards sex that have developed in the area deserve serious consideration as well. History of polygamous practices (at least for those who could afford it) and social construction of the Harem, as well as sexual slave-markets in Iran, have contributed to the formation of sexual meanings and the attitudes toward bartering of the body. Additionally, while the remainder of "harem culture" occupies the collective memory of people in Iran, the contemporary norms and social standards distinguish polygamy (as something that can be tolerated, even accepted under special circumstances) in contrast to obtaining sex-partners through slave markets and other similarly non-virtuous practices, like prostitution, deemed as sinful and corrupt. Nonetheless, from ancient times, human traffickers have been pirating bodies and taking them hostage for the purpose of slavery. Able bodies of captured men and women were used in order to build "great civilizations," to satisfy sexual desires of the dominant and the powerful. Much of scholarly research on human sexuality suggests the endurance of the tradition of sex-slavery since antiquated era. "The slave market had been a thriving commerce in the Middle East since Mesopotamian times, [where] young boys and girls captured in war or paid as tribute by their fathers or local rulers were available for purchase on the open market in all major cities" (Croutier, 1989:21).

Tracing back through Iranian textual history, one can find numerous references to *kanizakan* (female sex slaves) and *gholaman* (male slaves), who were brought in from expansionist wars or purchased at trade markets. The practice of taking up *kanizak*[3] into one's household continued ubiquitously throughout the region and was common practice in post-Islamic era. Although Iranian Islamic heritage celebrates the radical response of the Prophet to slavery[4], the adoption of female sex-slaves (*kanizak*) did not die off prior to the Pahlavi dynasty in Iran. As recent as 100 years ago, during the reign of the Qajar dynasty, women were frequently adopted into the King's court and prominent wealthy men, to work as domestic servants and to provide sex services to their masters. The recorded historical accounts suggests that majority of these women were captured from impoverished families in far away places—often from African continents—and sold off in slave markets (Nashat, 2004:37-60).

Conversely, within Shiite Islam and the Iranian adaptation of the faith, the institutionalism of temporary marriages or sigheh has legitimized marketing and bartering of the body. Sanctified under the rubric of the Prophet's Sunnat (life style and teachings), sigheh is strongly defended by many as a socially acceptable methodology for controlling and preventing prostitution. In Iran, while prostitution and the management of sex-trade remained illegal both prior to and after the political revolution of 1979, the ethical double-standard of forbidding the sale of the body by sex-workers while celebrating temporary (as short-term as a few hours) marriages in exchange for money has complicated responses to a growing social phenomenon. As early as 1934, Iran officially signed the 1921 International doctrine to prevent exploitation and bartering of women in or outside the country's geo-political borders (Kar, 1991:140).

"The freedom to choose one's mate is yet to be recognized and practiced by the public in Iran, especially among families of limited financial resources," writes Mehrangiz Kar, a former judge and an attorney specializing in family law, as well as a long time women's rights advocate in Iran (Kar, 2001:36). However, young girls from different regions in Iran experience a variety of limitations according to local cultures. Some of the earliest distinctions between genders begin with prohibiting young girls at pre-school level from playing in group games and sports, even disallowing their presence outside the house in the extremely traditional families. Many of the local cultures in the southern parts of Iran prohibit their young daughters to leave the house unescorted, even for grocery shopping, since popular belief understands this as a sign of weakness and the absence of authority of the man of the house. When a girl disobeys, her actions are rarely tolerated. In accordance with traditional values of the region, the male of her kin would respond tragically, and violently, in order to save face.

On the other hand, "children become the supporting pillars for the broken and shaky relations [in cases of domestic dispute]—a bait on a hook," writes Farzaneh Milani on the cultural significance of children within the family (Milani, 1992:196). Domestic services of these children are a necessity for many impoverished families. "Above all, woman's procreative power it seems remains insurance for mismatched alliances, with the failure to produce a child, preferably a boy, a cause for severe anxiety and desperation" (Milani, 1992:196). For families with limited financial resources, male children become additionally valuable as "Nan-avaran" or breadwinners. Young girls continue to simultaneously invoke sentiments of destitution (an additional mouth to feed), and to evoke the romantic notion of a future helping hand in the domestic realm. Prior to marriage, and especially among crowded families, daughters assume their domestic role in cooking and caring for the family at a very young age.

A daughter's participation in school, also, falls prey to cultural prejudice. Many of the Iranian girls in the south do not continue their education beyond elementary years, as their domestic assistance takes precedence over their education. Moreover, when they fall behind in their studies, the young girls are presumed lacking talent and intelligence. These harsh judgments about a girl's ability to learn and to excel in school are further utilized to argue the need to marry her off quickly. Despite an increase in women's participation in schools since the political revolution of 1979, the traditional notions of an ideal woman as someone "Najib" (innocent) and "Mojab" (agreeable) persists across social classes and ethnic groups. Images of the extreme polarization of women are reinforced through literature and culture, either as good mothers and caring wives that emphasizes their domestic service, or as promiscuous and transgressive bodies (i.e. "Lakateh," "Saliteh," "Faheshe," etc.). Numerous examples of such exist in the writings of great Persian cultural icons, from Saadi (the poet), to Amir Kabir (a social reformer), Hedayat (an intellectual pioneer) and beyond.

Similarly, with respect to the treatment of women by men, Iranian oral and textual history is frequently used to legitimize male dominance in contemporary culture. Much of the popular values are learned through proverbs and legendary stories passed on through continuous oral reiterations. Unfortunately, included in the oral culture of Iran are images of women as secondary to men, and descriptive teachings on how to train a woman into her proper obedient place. "There are many examples of women's lack of wit and wisdom in Iranian literal culture and legendary stories and poetry, which justify and reinforce the absolute authoritative position men assume over her" (Kar, 2001:42-43). Among them, Saadi, a prominent literary figure of the 12th century, and a "Master of Speech," offers an abundant collection of teachings on how to control a woman into submission:

در خرمی بر سرای یی ببند
که بانگ زن برآید وا از او بلند
. . .
زن خوب فرمانبر پارسا
کند مرد درویش را پادشاه

"Slam the door shut on a house
From which, the voice of a woman is heard"

. . .

"A good, obedient woman of character
Shall transform any ordinary (dervish) man into a king!"

When a man fails to demonstrate his absolute authority over his *Namous* (females of kin/sexual properties), he is harshly assessed in the public eye. In recent years, the metaphor of *zan-zalil* (wretched by women) has found itself a strong hold in public speech. A man who fails to demonstrate his absolute authority over his wife, is characterize by his friends (in the language of amusement, humor and sarcasm) as a miserable man, a *zan-zalil*.

On a more philosophical level, Iranians often assign a positive value to the notions of patience (*Sabr*) and destiny (*bakht*) as Islamic virtues. When confronted with circumstances of extreme injustices, the language of God's supreme power and wisdom in choosing one's *ghesmat*, or as Abu-Lughod calls it, her "divinely decreed lot in life" (Abu-Lughod, 1988:271), is taken on both as a coping mechanism and a point of legitimacy. At the same time, it must be noted that concepts of *ghesmat* (one's destiny) and its counter-part *masouliat* (religious and social responsibility to confront injustices) are frequently contended in juxtaposition of one another, and their application fluctuates depending upon specific circumstances. In relation to the problem of sex trafficking in southern areas of Iran, the role of education about multiple applications of cultural and spiritual concepts in terms of attitudes toward life in contemporary situations acquires a significant value. While achieving such objectives (to educate the public in order to reverse their cultural attitudes) may seem out of reach, we are reminded by the massive fluctuations that women in Iran have endured in a historically short period of time, since the Constitutional Revolution of 1906-09. Writing on the significant shifts in the conception of women as mothers and wives, belonging to the house ("Manzil"), to "managers of the house (Muddabir-i manzil)," Najmabadi points out the role of education and new formulation of traditional values at the time:

> The new regulatory practices and concepts defined the acceptable social space for freedom for the modern woman . . . . Thus women constituted at once a new individual self through literacy and a new social self through patriotic political activities. As managers of the house, they were beginning to transform "the house" into a social space of citizenship (Najmabadi, 1998:113-114).

Final Remarks

New trends of sex-trade in the Gulf region have emerged out of a cluster of cultural and social matters, with their roots in the political history of the people in the area. An accelerating poor economy for the majority of people in Iran, impoverished living situations, and a failure to educate the public about the value and rights of women, are a few of the contributing factors that make up the social/political constellation resulting in the thriving market of human and sex trafficking. In terms of market economy, sex workers and human trafficking circles often expand their activities over areas where the demand for bartering the body is high and an overflow of clientele is assured. In part, the increase in demands for an underground sex-market in Dubai can be attributed to the continuous military presence in the Gulf region due to multiple wars of the last few decades. Such direct correlations between the brothel industry and the presence of military forces in the area, is neither new nor exclusive to the Middle East. However, the increase in trafficking of Iranian girls into Dubai is directly linked to the recent transformation of the city as a geopolitically significant and economically flourishing hub in the Gulf region. Mass-migrations caused by a constellation of political revolutions and war, resurgence of religious fundamentalism, and the return of traditional cultural values towards gender provide a new niche for sex-trade to go underground, and for new money to be poured into its industry. There is a steadfast commerce driving the transport of sex workers through the Dubai-gate and into the International market. "Networks of prostitution transfer runaway girls to the Arabian countries of the Persian Gulf through the aid of powerful venture capitalists and business enterprises, which make large payments necessary to obtain official documentations and visas for these girls" (Intekhab, 2002). To confront the growth of sex-trade, on the one hand, requires a substantial awareness and possible collaborations with the powerful industry that responds to this market.

On the other hand, uncontested local traditions and sexually violent views of women that persist in the region have created a breeding ground for human trafficking and underground sex trade endeavors. A sustainable program to educate the public about new attitudes toward women and sex is the other important course of actions. However, it is equally insufficient to presume that an extensive public educational program alone will eradicate the problem of human-trafficking commerce in the area. For people to participate in educational programs and to adopt a new life style, they need to have alternative methods of generating income. In other words, for people living in poverty, the extent of agency—in terms of control over circumstances of their lives—is constrained and restricted[5]. In short, to understand, critique, and prevent further exploitation of women and children in the smuggling circles of the Persian Gulf, a multi-disciplinary perspective that goes beyond the traditional political economy of the trade is necessary.

References

Abu-Lughod, Lila. (1998) *Remaking women, feminism and modernity in the Middle East.* Princeton, NJ: Princeton University Press.

Anderson, Benedict. (1991) *Imagined communities: Reflections on the origin and Spread of nationalism.* New York: Verso. (First four chapters).

Aref News, (November 5, 2005) Reported in *Integration forum der Iraniannen in Deutschland* (web-based news site). November 8, 2005. http://www.if-id.de/report/

Croutier, Alev Lytle. (1989) *Harem: The world behind the veil.* NY: Abbeville Press.

Farmer, P.E., et al., (2001) "Community-based approaches to HIV treatment in resource-poor settings." *The Lancet* 358(9279): p. 404-9

Farzam, Parichehr. (2006) Special report in Radio Liberty. July 6, 2006. http://www.radiofarda.com/iran_article/2006/06/7

Ghanbarpour, Sina. 29 December 2003) "The Absence of Security in Bam." In Shargh Newspaper. 1(101).

http://www.sharghnewspaper.com/821008/disast.htm

Hunter, M. (2002) The materiality of everyday sex: thinking beyond 'prostitution'. African Studies, 61(1): p. 99-120. "Special report on prostitution rings in Dubai." (23 May 2002) The sociology page in *Intekhab*.

Kar, Mehrangiz. (2001) *A research about violence against women in Iran.* Roshangaran Puplishers. Tehran, Iran.

Kar, Mehrangiz. (1999) *Eliminating discrimination against women: Comparing the convention on elimination of all forms of discrimination against women to the Iranian legislation.* Parvin/Ghatreh Publications. Tehran, Iran.

Milani, Farzaneh. (1992) *Veils and words: The emerging voices of Iranian women writers.* Syracuse, NY: Syracuse University Press.

Najmabadi, Afsaneh. (1998) *Remaking women, feminism and modernity in the Middle East*. Edited by In Abu-Lughod, Lila. Princeton, NJ: Princeton University Press.

Nashat, Guity. (2004) "Marriage in Qajar Period" in Women in Iran: from 1800 to the Islamic Republic. Lois Beck and Guity Nashat. University of Illinois Press.

Rafizadeh, Shahram. (2005) "Selling bodies of Iranian girls in Dubai," in Integration Forum der Iraniannen in Deutschland (web-based news site). http://www.if-id.de/report/February2006/Tanforushi.php

Rice, Condoleezza. (2006) "Victims of trafficking and violence protection act of 2000." Released by the Office to Monitor and Combat Trafficking in Persons—US Department of State—June 5, 2006. http://www.state.gov/g/tip/rls/tiprpt/2006/

Shahrokhi, Sholeh. 2001. Field Journal, unpublished writing. Book I.

Three

FROM THAILAND WITH LOVE:
TRANSNATIONAL MARRIAGE MIGRATION
IN THE GLOBAL CARE ECONOMY

Sine Plambech

Introduction

Transnational brides are just one segment of the 60 million female migrants of today. During the 1970s, Western Europe and Australia were common destinations for South-East Asian brides (De Stoop, 1994). In the 1980s and 1990s, migration movements diversified to include women from Latin America, Mexico, China and the Philippines who traveled to the USA, as well as women migrating from Eastern to Western Europe (Kojima, 2001). Historically, women have always migrated. The apparent tendency of feminization in global migration can be explained both by the number of female migrants as well as by gender-specific reasons for migration. Based on ethnographic fieldwork with a group of Thai women and Danish men, this article seeks to contribute new perspectives to the so called mail order bride discourse, as well as to perceptions of transnational marriages between women from Thailand and European men.

The existing discourse has categorized mail-order brides, in a non-critical but problematic manner, as victims. This non-contemporary perception has its roots in the universalist feminist discourse of the 1970s, in which marriage was essentially considered as being suppressive, regardless of the woman's own experience and opinions. The assumption that the woman was a victim, and unaware of her suppression, was particularly applied to women from third world countries (Constable, 2003, p.6).

This discussion is interesting in relation to Thai women, in view of their status as foreigners who come from a third world country in order to enter into marriage. Here, the same mechanisms that are considered suppressive in the universalist feminist discourse are incorporated into one and the same woman, making it hardly surprising that mail order brides are considered to be victims. However, these perceptions represent a distorted picture and are, to put it bluntly, rooted in non-contemporary perceptions of sexual inequality and the intrinsic subservience of the female sex. They can be seen as an expression of a patriarchal view of sexuality that keeps women in the role of the victim and does not differentiate between will and force (ibid.).

Five significant themes have characterized this discourse until now, in both a Danish and international context: First, the woman is considered a victim of illegal trafficking.[1] The link between transnational marriages and trafficking arises from perceptions of women from abroad who are specifically bought as marriage partners by western men. This commercial perspective is reminiscent of prostitution, and should be examined critically as it tends to have no relation to reality. Thai brides are not a commodity that men purchase and consume (Schaeffer-Grabiel, 2004, p.33).

Second, Thai women are perceived as victims of violence. The National Association of Women's' Crisis Centers in Denmark (LOKK, 2003) has documented that those Asian women who most frequently visit a Danish crisis center are Thais (p.13). Due to language barriers, lack of knowledge about Danish legislation and, in some cases, a weak social network, women are particularly vulnerable to the consequences of the husband's violence (ibid. p.3). These conditions justify the perception of the women in question as victims. However, the violence aspect is also promoted by media portraying these marriages in a sensationalist manner that exclusively focuses on negative cases of Danish men who make a habit of marrying and divorcing Thai women, or by citing extreme examples of violence and abuse (Julag-Ay, as cited in Constable, 2003, p.86). There is little knowledge about Thai women in Denmark as many spend all their time in the home and are provided for by their husbands. As "self providers," these women are able to avoid almost all contact with public authorities (from an interview with the Nykøbing-Mors employment exchange). This phenomenon gives rise to two problems, the first being that exploitation and violence can remain unnoticed and concealed within the home, while the other is that common knowledge of Thai women and their marriages is primarily based on information from women who have been in contact with a crisis center precisely because they have been subjected to violence. Knowledge about the lives of Thai women in Denmark and transnational marriages that succeed without violence is limited. Nonetheless, it is essential in order to reveal the deeper reasons for such marriages and the conflicts that can arise.

Third, there is a perception that these women have "burnt all their bridges"[2] and therefore represent a vulnerable group without a social network in Denmark or ties to their country of origin. The Thai women in this study, however, have both a social network and connections with their families in Thailand—an aspect that this article seeks to illustrate. Glick Schiller, Basch & Blanc-Szanton (1995) have already demonstrated how migrants are often characterized as uprooted, or disconnected from their country of origin due to their migration (p. 48). In a watershed article (1995), they argue in favor of a more complex understanding of the migrant concept. Characterizing migrants who retain and sustain their ties to their country of origin more precisely as transmigrants.

Fourth, a general case of gender blindness in migrant theory has ignored the fact that women can and will migrate for other reasons than those of men. In the case of the Thai women's migration and marriages, this can be illustrated by the wish of the family in Thailand for her to marry a foreign man at the same time as the woman herself wants to liberate herself from the traditional gender roles of Thai society.

Fifth, rather than embracing a global economic perspective, the discourse beyond the four themes outlined above has primarily explained these marriages as a result of extreme poverty, or the need of Danish men for control and sexual services. By placing these women's own perspectives at the focal point of the analysis and linking these to the wider influence of global processes, it is my intention to introduce new aspects to the mail order bride discourse in a Danish context.

Initially, I will present the ethnographic context, followed by a care-economic analysis of transnational marriages on a macro level, and then proceed to demonstrate how a transnational network supports these marriages. Subsequently, I will link the care-economic perspective with the motives of these women and their husbands for entering into marriage at the individual micro level.

Chutima, Kita, Siriporn, and Peter[3]

My focus for the discussion in this paper is Jens, a young Danish man married to a Thai, and three young Thai women from northeastern Thailand.[4] The women, Chutima, Kita, and Siriporn, are all married, or have previously been married, to a Danish husband. They describe themselves as Thai girls. The interviews with the three women have been selected from a series of interviews supplemented by private visits, visits to companies, meetings with the employment exchange and the language school. As is the case with most anthropological studies in complex societies, this study is qualitative and local, enabling it to highlight new perspectives and contribute to a differentiated understanding of this type of transnational marriage. It cannot, however, be a basis for generalization.

The geographical locality of this study is northwest rural Denmark. There is a general tendency towards large groups of Asian women in rural areas, particularly in Australia and the USA (Ehrenreich & Hochschild, 2002; Pettman, 1996; Constable, 2003). In Scandinavia, the number of transnational marriages in rural areas is growing. This growth is often accounted for by a lack of women, especially younger women, which, as often as not, is due to increasing demand for female labor in urban areas. Isolated workplaces in a local setting that primarily use male labor also contributes to making it difficult for men to meet local women (Cahill, 1990, p.67). One reason for the women in this study to live in rural Denmark was that they knew other Thai women already married to Danes in this area.

Jens lives on Mors, a small island in the region of northwest Denmark, and is married to Chutima, with whom he has a small daughter. They live in a new detached bungalow in a small village, and they both work in the fish processing industry—Jens more than full-time, while Chutima works eight hours a week. Chutima has lived in Denmark for five years. She has an aunt who helped her and five cousins to come to the Mors area in Denmark. In Thailand, Chutima grew up as the only girl in the family together with her two brothers. She later worked 16 hours a day in a factory making air-conditioning parts for export.

Siriporn is divorced, has two daughters, and rents an apartment in a small provincial town. She owns a house that she rents out. Siriporn grew up with her parents and eight siblings in a village to the north east of Bangkok. From the age of 16 she worked in a chicken slaughterhouse and in a supermarket. Siriporn has lived in Denmark for 11 years and has two marriages with Danish men behind her. She has an older sister in the city of Aarhus, in Denmark, who introduced her to each of her Danish husbands. Siriporn's younger sister came to Denmark in 2004. She lives on the other side of the street and is married to a mutual acquaintance of Siriporn and her older sister in Aarhus. Siriporn is on welfare after an accident at work, but has had her own restaurant for some years where she serves Thai food.

Kita has lived in Denmark for four years. She is a friend of Siriporn and both women come from the same area of Thailand. Kita worked in a factory in northern Thailand. She is now married to a friend of Siriporn's ex-husband and looks after the home. The couple lives in a rented apartment and has no children. Kita goes to Danish classes twice a week at a language school in a larger nearby town.

Many Thai women in the area are unemployed, look after the home, or work in the fish processing industry. The latter involves keeping up a fast pace on a production line, cleaning and packing fish and mussels. The employees call their workplaces "The Mussel" or "The Fish." Many of the Thai women have had similar jobs in Thailand and have no further education as exemplified by Chutima's, Siriporn's and Kita's backgrounds. The opposite applies in the case of Russian women married to Danes. These women generally have a higher education, while Thai women in Denmark generally have no education beyond basic schooling (LOKK, 2003, p. 12). The employment exchange officer in Nykøbing Mors pointed out that jobs in the fish processing plant matched the previous work experience of the Thai women, and met the labor requirement in fish processing factories that still operate conventional production lines and suffer from a lack of Danish female labor.

Chutima, Kita, and Siriporn did not find their husbands via the Internet or in a catalog. The meeting with them indicates that the term mail order brides has troublesome implications: the main reason being that the women and married couples that I met had not been introduced by mail order. On the contrary, they had met via local personal networks, via women and men who were already married to a Danish husband or Thai woman. They had exchanged a few letters after which the man sent an air ticket and the couple met in Denmark. Glodava and Onizuka (1994) defined mail order brides as women who find their partners via correspondence. This process can be initiated by a marriage agency, a catalog, a newspaper, or by friends or family. The juxtaposition of a formal marriage agency and personal family contacts is problematic. First, there are significantly different social factors involved when contacts are made via a personal network. Secondly, the women do not see themselves as, or have no knowledge of the concept of, a mail order bride. Sociologist Cecilia Julag-Ay points out that the term is of little use as it is not value-neutral, and, moreover, has "many negative connotations" (As cited in Constable, 2003, p. 70).

Care Economics in Denmark

Knowledge of this type of transnational marriage has been characterized by studies undertaken before the woman or man had decided to marry, or after some marriages had ended in violence. The most quoted book on the subject is *Mail-Order Brides: Women for Sale* by Mila Glodava and Richard Onizuka (1994). In the book, they summarize the discourse up until then, which was characterized by generalizations and uncritical dichotomies between strong men who buy brides and suppressed women who sell themselves. Since then, Nicole Constable (2003) has performed virtual ethnography among American men and women in a study of how identities are constructed in the internet based on the wish to find a matching partner. Constable's analysis contributes an anthropological perspective and a feminist criticism that refutes Glodava and Onizuka's approach, overlooks central distinctions while also underestimating the ability of women to make informed and rational choices. Yu Kojima (2001) also employs virtual ethnography among Korean women migrating to Japan to argue that this group of female migrants should be seen as reproductive working migrants who perform domestic and reproductive work that Japanese women no longer wish to do (p. 205). This is a perspective to which I will return.

Research in recent years generally points to the fact that the women who migrate to the West for marriage purposes have a complex set of motives, and, more often than not, make their decision on the basis of a number of factors. For this reason, these women should not be uncritically categorized as victims of illegal trafficking. Research demonstrates first and foremost that marginalized women in a marginalized economy can and will create strategies for controlling their economic lives (Kojima, 2002; Constable, 2003; (Bloch, 2003; Schaeffer-Grabiel, 2004; Sassen, 2002; Ehrenreich and Hochschild, 2002). Few have focused on how marriages at the macro level can be analyzed in the light of wider global processes, in which care is an export commodity that is exchanged by means of a visa and monthly economic payments to the family back at home (cf. Ehrenreich and Hochchild, 2002; Sassen, 2002). The economic exchange is thus more complex than a commercial perspective in which the woman enters into marriage as the result of an illegal transaction, or in which the husband-to-be pays an agency, the woman, or her family for the marriage. Nor do the women migrate because of extreme poverty. They could quite easily survive purely physically in Thailand; their existence is not under threat. They act on the basis of a relatively recently felt poverty as a result of the economic crisis in Thailand at the end of the 1990s (ESCAP, 1999, p.13). Glick Schiller et al. (1995) also points out that it is not the poor who migrate of their own volition, as migrating requires resources in all classes of society. Migration is often a strategy for making sure that a household unit is able to retain its assets in the form of resources and social standing (p. 48-54).

The Thai currency was devalued in July, 1997, triggering a widespread economic crisis in Asia. The lower middle class and the poor in Thailand were especially vulnerable, and in 1998, the unemployment rate accelerated as a result of factory closures and dismissals (ESCAP, 1999, p. 13). It is generally acknowledged that such a series of events and actions impacts women, as they are usually responsible for the health of the family and their children's education. This responsibility is the main explanation behind the global rise in the number of female migrants who travel in order to help their families in their country of origin by sending money to them. All of the Thai girls in this study send money every month to Thailand. Siriporn explains the situation like this:

> We are not poor in my family, but we do not have a lot of money. This is why my sister and I send an amount of 500 Danish kroner [corresponding to about 75 US dollars] every month to our family . . . That was really why we came [to Denmark]. My brothers in Thailand do not have spare cash to send to our parents.

The Thai girls make no secret of the fact that they send money back to Thailand. Money remittances from migrants to their countries of origin are not a new phenomenon, but merely a growing one. Studies of migrant cash remittances have, however, focused primarily on remittances from rich to poor countries. Luis Eduardo Guarnizo (2003) suggests that this approach is a simplification, as it does not take account of the macro-economic effects of a transnational migrant economy, thus underestimating the migrant influence on the global economy (p. 667).

Structural limitations arise from phenomena that impact the specific living conditions of the women and their families. By migrating and marrying, these women seek to challenge and push back these limitations. This is currently manifest by the growth in variation of what Saskia Sassen (2002) calls alternative global circuits for survival and profit making. These circuits embrace a rising number of women. The most central of these circuits include illegal trafficking, nannies, servant girls and transnational brides. Another perspective is the development strategy of the country of origin that can motivate its citizens to look for work, or find other ways of improving their economic situation by migrating (Sassen 2002, para. 4). This can take place officially, as is the case in the Philippines where the government ran an information campaign to get Philippine women to marry Japanese men, thus helping their families back home. It can also take place unofficially, as in Thailand where a remittance economy and bridal migration is a cornerstone strategy towards the underprivileged, as illustrated by Chutima:

> Almost all the girls I know in Thailand want to leave. Many girls from my village have also left. Now they leave the country directly from the village as there are many Thai girls around the world who are willing to help them. They do not need to go to Pattaya[5] first to find a husband. These girls travel to the USA, Germany, Norway, or the UK.

These women—and often migrants in general—are thus part of a macro-level development strategy. Marriage and a residence permit in Denmark open the door for countless money transfers from these women to their families in their country of origin. Many countries regard these remittances as a valuable international currency resource. In 1998, global remittances between migrants and their countries of origin amounted to 70 billion US dollars (Sassen 2002, ¶ 3). By migrating and regularly sending money, these brides are thus part of an alternative global circuit.

Sassen's economic analysis of the function of female migrants can be linked to the care drain concept of Ehrenreich and Hochschilds (2003).[6] This concept highlights the global contexts that have contributed to the rise in the number of remittances by migrants, increasingly women, who leave their own families to take care of others. These new, global care circuits are an important, but frequently overlooked, consequence of "globalization." They arise from the importation of care, love, and service by rich countries, and the exportation of female migrants from poor countries to perform these care and service functions. Care drain manifests itself primarily as a private, and thus almost invisible, phenomenon. In Denmark, it is represented by the many "self-supporting" Thai girls who look after the home. Another type of care that is in demand is for sexual services, which are increasingly being offered by female migrants. Marriages with women from abroad is thus just one phenomenon of care import, and Ehrenreich points out that care import is just one more resource that is being extracted from poor countries to rich ones (p. 6).

Kita, Siriporn, and Chutima have no children in Thailand, but many of their cousins and girlfriends in Denmark do. This is not unusual as many Thai girls leave their children in Thailand when they marry in Denmark. Siriporn explains that her mother looks after the grandchildren left behind by Siriporn's sisters when they migrated.

The concepts and phenomena of global care chains, care drain, and alternative global circuits for survival and profit making can be united in the concept of the global care economy. The global care economy can be seen in rural Denmark, where women have left their own children and elderly parents to marry and care for Danish men. When Chutima goes to the bank every month to send 150 US dollars to her parents in northern Thailand, she is literally living out her role as a player in a global care economy.

A Transnational Network

Transmigrants are defined as migrants whose daily life depends on constant and highly diverse connections across international borders. Transnational migration is a process in which migrants create and sustain simultaneous and many-facetted social relations that connect their country of origin with their country of residence (Glick Schiller, et.al, 1995, p. 48). Chutima, Kita, and Siriporn have a number of relations in Denmark who, as a whole, make up a central network for the Thai girls. This network also functions as a relation that connects the country of origin with their country of residence. This finding thus refutes general perceptions of migrants as being alienated from their countries of origin. The monthly remittances and the network in Denmark both demonstrate that the Thai girls cannot be considered as being uprooted or as having "burnt all their bridges."

My aunt was the first to leave, settling in Denmark when I was a small girl. She met her husband through her work in Pattaya. My aunt called me from Denmark and told me about a man from work who wanted to marry a Thai girl. She has since found a husband for my five cousins and they now all live in this area. Once one girl arrives, she can arrange for the rest of the women in her family to come. One of my friends has ten sisters and cousins here (Chutima).

The network shows that the role of the woman as a player in the global care economy has a number of implications. Not only must she send money home, but she can also help more girls to come who can then also send money home. The lower practical costs of migrating due to an active network in Denmark increase the number of women who can choose to leave, thus it can be argued that migration networks increase the number of migrants in a cumulative process (Massey, 1988); (Light nd& Bhachu, 1993, p.27). The women and their families in Thailand see these marriages as an opportunity to consolidate what Schaeffer-Grabiel calls a transborder middle-class identity (2004, p.42). First, this identity is pinned on the Thai girls in Denmark by their families and social network in Thailand. The Thai girls are considered as part of the middle class in Denmark, even though they may not be so in reality. Second, the family in Thailand acquires access to sustain its position as part of the middle class in their own locality. Thus the migration of their family member offers them social mobility. Chutima recounts that her big dream is to buy or build a house for her parents in Thailand. The result so far is the purchase of a television, refrigerator, and a washing machine for her parents when Chutima has visited them in Thailand. "Dollar houses" are houses paid for and built by the transnational remittances of migrants. They are becoming increasingly common in Asia, the Caribbean, Latin America, and Africa, and are influencing the price of land (Glick Schiller, et al., 1995, p. 54). Thus "dollar houses" demonstrate the necessity of studying and analyzing migration in both a transnational and a global economic perspective.

The network as a social institution in northwest Denmark is not an isolated geographical unit, as many Thai girls know other Thai girls who are married in Denmark and Europe. Neither is it specifically organized, structured, or even defined as a "network" by the Thai girls. "We just help each other," as Kita says. The network is an active participant in the migration process itself, but also functions as a social institution that brings together the Thai girls in the area, demonstrating that not all Thai girls are part of a fragile group without a social network. Yet the network is a social forum in which conflicts between the Thai girls are a central element. Kita explains:

> Even though we help each other, conflicts often arise because of jealousy. For example, if someone has more than someone else, like a good husband or a bigger house. We are nasty to each other and call each other whores . . . I often have problems with my cousins, but mostly with friends . . . we always help our own families most . . . I have helped a number of girls to come here [to Denmark], but I only do so if I know the man well. Otherwise the girls will be mad at me if they have problems when they come.

Good men who are recommended as husbands-to-be are those who, according to the Thai girls, let the girls stay at home, who don't hit them, and who make sure there is enough money for the family in Thailand. Simultaneously, the family in Thailand does not wait passively for the monthly remittances. They are also part of the transnational network. Glick Schiller calls this overlapping of functions flexible, extended family networks, which are not a new phenomenon. These networks are the basis for what Glick Schiller call collective transnational family strategies, indicating how the networks cross national boundaries, and how families thus acquire the opportunity to achieve economic security. Because the decision to migrate is closely linked to the opportunity to transfer money to the family in Thailand, the family joins the network in Denmark as part of the transnational network. For the Thai girls, free will is thus not necessarily a free choice between a number of economic alternatives, as they are in Denmark to fulfill important economic needs within a specific social and family context.

Marriage as an Individual Project

Personal choices and dreams of freedom, along with motherhood and love, are motives for migration at the micro-level. These are choices that must, however, be seen in the context of the structural frameworks and limited opportunities that are inherent in growing up in societies that have their own ways of prompting women to transnational marriages. An analysis that focuses on the women, and to a certain extent the men, illustrates how they, like most other people, are part of a social network; they seek to control their own conditions of life, that they exert power, and are also the object of power exerted by others. The motives demonstrate that women migrate for different reasons than men, a perspective that it is necessary to include in contemporary migration theory. I have demonstrated how women migrate in order to contribute to the family and thus fulfill an expected family duty. Simultaneously, migration can also be a process of liberation from the family. Migration as a freedom project is a complex field where apparently conflicting actions meet. Thai women migrate and enter into transnational marriages in order to express western ideas about freedom and individuality. These ideas, however, exist side by side with traditional perceptions of family values, gender roles, and femininity. Thus these intimate links and marriages incorporate perceptions of both the traditional and modern, and the global and local (Schaeffer-Grabiel, 2004, p. 45).

There are three central factors for the Thai girls in an analysis of individual motives for migration and marriage: freedom from harsh working conditions, freedom from Thai gender roles, and their ideas about Danish men. In the first case, Chutima, Kita, and Siriporn all worked up to 16 hours a day, six days a week, in a factory in Thailand. In Denmark, Kita looks after the house and her husband goes out to work. Siriporn has stayed at home looking after the children for long periods of her marriage, and Chutima works only eight hours a week, spending the rest of her time in the home where she does the cleaning and cooking. Her husband, Jens, works late every day. All of the women see a man as good if he lets his wife stay at home. This contrasts with a specific perception of suppression and exploitation that is often linked to these marriages, where the women who stay at home are perceived as suppressed regardless of their own experience and opinions. This perception has its roots in a western, feministic, middle-class vision of equality that criticizes families with a specific private/public work division where the husband works outside the home, while the woman stays at home. This criticism of gender roles in marriage often lacks an acknowledgement of the fact that women in different socio-cultural contexts define equality in different ways. Constable (2003) makes the point precisely:

> To work for a wage might be liberating to a middle-class woman, but not to a woman who has worked in fields or a factory for subsistence since childhood (p. 65).

Hence, even though Kita, Siriporn, and Chutima stay home and look after the house, this is not necessarily an expression of passivity or suppression.

Second, all of the Thai girls talked about nighttime trips to discotheques in the nearby town because they could go out in the evening and dance in Denmark. It is generally accepted in Denmark that married women can do these things, but the Danish husbands of the Thai girls often do not accept it. This is not what they were looking for, and the phenomenon explains why jealousy is a major cause of marital problems. Siriporn explains:

> Many Thai girls are married to older men. The Thai girls are young, they go to discotheques and cheat on their husbands, even though their husbands are good to them . . . It's because Denmark is free . . . Many Thai girls have several men in Denmark. They can't do that in Thailand, but here in Denmark she is free to do what she wants.

New studies of women seeking marriage in the West demonstrate that the women are also influenced by imaginary fantasies about western ideals of freedom and a liberating life style (Schaeffer-Grabiel, 2004, p. 34). Linked to this idea of seeking freedom is the third important motive for marriage, especially for women who do not already have children in Thailand. This springs from a dream of fulfilling a role as mother and wife, a dream that the women do not believe they can actualize in Thailand for fear of violence and alcohol abuse in the marriage. They preferred Danish husbands because they have a reputation among Thai girls for not drinking and beating their wives, as well as for letting their wives play a bigger role in marital decisions. Danish men were preferred to Thai men, whom the girls described as poor, out of work, dominating, drunk, violent and unfaithful. Strikingly, many female migrants have left violent husbands with alcohol abuse (Ehrenreich et al., 2002) including a number of those I met. It is not my purpose to ignore the fact that many have been subjected to violence and abuse, but by describing Thai men as dominating and morally depraved, the women divert a moralizing discourse away from perceptions and accusations that the Thai girls who marry Danish husbands are the ones who are prostitutes and morally depraved. Transnational brides from Asia, Colombia, Russia, and Mexico have also justified their search and marriage with men from other countries by denigrating men from their own countries (Del Rosario, 1994). This illustrates how these marriages can be understood as a personal and national sexual revolution on a transnational level (Schaeffer-Grabiel 2004, p. 40). Even though the women apply this discourse, they do not entertain discussion of the possibility that the same structural conditions and lack of economic opportunity that influenced their own migration may also influence the opportunities for Thai men to be economically stable caretakers.

The stories told by the Thai girls were often contradictory. They described Danish men as dominating, while underlining the desirability of Thai family values, such as loyalty and the well-defined role of the Thai man as a care-er. The contrasting constructions from the Thai girls of men from Denmark and Thailand illustrate how it is not only the women who are seen as objects and categorized as traditional, erotic, and passive. Danish men are also seen as objects, as symbols of attractive, alternative ways of living on the basis of their nationality. Thus the migration and marriages of the Thai girls are linked to individual dreams about the good life, wealth, independence, love, motherhood, and of liberation from Thai gender roles, which the Danish husband paradoxically hopes to import. The quest of men for women from abroad is a quest for a "sweet" and faithful girl with traditional family values. These are family values that men nostalgically believe existed in the 1950s before other family constellations than the nuclear family emerged (Schaeffer-Grabiel, 2004, p. 40). The men want to import sex, care, and love, but also have the idea that they are importing women with firmly anchored traditions. Jens explains:

> I think many Thai girls come because men without wives look at men who have a Thai wife and think "I'd like one of those, too." They may also find it difficult to score real Danish women and end up with the one they want. Danish women can be difficult and complicated . . . they make some big demands.

The men also nurture considerably greater romantic aspirations when it comes to marriage than the women. Jens continues:

> I met a nice Thai girl in the packing room at work. She was married to a Dane and I asked her whether she might know another nice Thai girl, or maybe she had a sister. She got in touch with her niece, now my wife, in Thailand and I sent two letters to her. Understanding each other was difficult by letter. There's not a lot to write about and my English isn't too good. So I enclosed an air ticket in my third letter. I thought that if it didn't work out she could just enjoy it as a holiday and then return home. I went to Copenhagen airport to pick her up. I was terribly nervous before she arrived. I can't really explain how I felt, but it was like having butterflies in my stomach.

Contrasting expectations produce conflicting results (Schaeffer-Grabiel, 2004, p. 45), especially because Danish men hope to establish traditional family and gender values, while some of the Thai girls want to transcend them. This explains why there are instructions on the Internet about how to tackle a woman from Thailand, Russia, or the Philippines. Not least, it also offers a possible explanation of conflicts that can lead to marital violence. The marriage and the women are often far from what the men imagine. The woman is not just a "sweet" girl, but an independent individual. Conflicts arise when two worlds of imagination meet in a collision between two conflicting projects: care versus visa.

Conclusion

This article criticizes the existing "mail-order bride" discourse, while seeking to extend and deepen it. Initially, five significant themes in the existing discourse were outlined that were rooted in an explicit victim perspective. I have demonstrated that the marriage and migration of women have causes rooted in far more complex motives than controlling men who buy poverty-stricken women. This simple commercial perspective is anchored in a problematic, essentialist, and universalist feministic approach that ignores the women's own perspective and power of action.

Part of the theoretical and analytical approach of the article is thus linked to more recent feminist studies of prostitution and sexual services. Like mail order brides, prostitutes are also frequently described as slaves, as trafficked, and as victims (Constable, 2003, p. 89), despite the fact that many women working in the Asian sex industry point out that prostitution should be seen in another perspective: as a job in a well-defined industry, as a survival strategy, or as a way of getting by in the absence of other options (Kempadoo, as cited in Constable, 2003, p. 89). Despite the marginalization and vulnerability inherent in Asian prostitution, the role of the victim is rejected both by prostitutes themselves and in studies based on the perspective of the prostitutes themselves. Neither did the Thai girls see themselves as victims, either of male control or of poverty. How should we interpret the way marginalized women see their own situation? As an expression of "false awareness" with Danish-married Thai girls being seen as victims despite their own perception? Or is it possible to accept and includes the women's own perception in a future discourse? Kamala Kempadoo asks for increased attention to the agency of marginalized women through acknowledgement of their role as players in the global arena and by seeing their individual decisions as conscious and rational reactions to structurally determined conditions. By placing the women in the center of analyses that include the women's own perceptions, Kempadoo argues in favor of an innovative reinterpretation of prostitution in the Third World (Ibid., p. 89). In the same way, a reinterpretation and extension of the existing "mail order bride" discourse is possible by focusing on the women themselves and listening to their own perceptions.

In this article, Chutima's, Siriporn's, and Kita's personal perceptions and experiences have contributed to a deeper understanding of Thai-Danish marriages, and illustrated

49

migration as a specific action performed by individuals in a specific socio-cultural context. The parallel inclusion of a global perspective demonstrates that the migration and marriages of the Thai girls is a complex mixture of free will, necessity and force. It is also important to underline the fact that focus of the agency of the women does not mean that their lives as migrant women are without problems or that their migration is not rooted in fundamental gender inequalities. As already pointed out, migration theory has, in general, not implemented a gender perspective despite the fact that women want to, can, and must migrate for other reasons than men.

Anti-trafficking organizations often cite mail order brides as a target group.[7] The critical point is the extent to which the women voluntarily entered into the marriage, and to what extent she had been paid for. As I have already demonstrated, both free will and economy are complex concepts in relation to the migration of the Thai girls. Secondly, significant distinctions between groups of migrating women are often overlooked, as prostitutes, sex slaves, housekeepers, and mail order brides are all characterized as victims of trafficking (Constable, 2003, p. 214). While the differences between the various groups of migrant women can be indistinct and perhaps form a continuum rather than a series of discrete categories, finer distinctions are important. Saskia Sassen pinpoints the problem of the uncritically linking of mail order brides to trafficking, as this blurs their participation in transnational migration, as well as the fact that they make a significant contribution to a global remittance and care economy. The complex realities, structural limitations, and global processes that influence the choice of these women is overlooked when mail order brides are linked to trafficking. At the same time, the women's ability to take personal decisions and perform economic strategies is underestimated (Guarnizo, 2003, p. 667).

Some women are victims of trafficking, and are ignorant of the potential dangers of migration in terms of violence and exploitation. The women I met were both knowledgeable about structural conditions in a wider context that made them choose migration, and about the potential danger of violence and complications when migrating to a new country. The structural limitations and mechanisms that influence the woman and the life of her family are considered more dangerous than potential violence. By migrating, these women react primarily to their feeling of social exclusion and the fear of economic discrimination, both of themselves and of their family. Thus, the Thai girls are not victims. On the contrary, they are independent and dependent, resourceful, exploiting and exploited at the same time. With this more pragmatic player perspective as the point of departure, the second part of the theoretical and analytical approach of this article is founded in recent feminist analyses of the role of female migrants in the global economy. The new global care circuits are a frequently overlooked consequence of globalization. The dominant globalization discourse concentrates on major capital transactions, seldom on smaller, private remittances. This, however, means underestimating the function of migrant women in the global economy. On the other hand, if we expand the narrative of globalization, we can include care and service as commercial commodities that are exported from poor to rich countries—care and service that support global dynamics and the global economy. Marriage migration is just an example of a concrete manifestation of care exporting. By analyzing the marriages in a care perspective, I have argued for considering the Thai girls in rural Denmark as players in a global care economy.

References

Bloch, A. (2003). "Trafficking in the Russian Far East: Dreams of Prosperity and Discourses on Danger. Paper presented at the conference: The International Migration of "Traditional Women." International Conference at the Centre for Comparative Immigration Studies: University of California, San Diego.

Buckser, A. S. (1996). *Communities of Faith—Sectarianism, Identity and Social Change on a Danish Island*. Berghahn Books.

Cahill, D. (1990). *Intermarriages in International Contexts*. Australia: Scalabrini Migration Centre.

Carøe Christiansen, C. (2001). *Kvinders islamiske aktivisme i et transnationalt perspektiv. Dansk Sociologi*, 4, 8-21.

Constable, N. (2003). *Romance on a Global Stage*. Berkeley: University of California Press.

Del Rosario, V. (1994). Lifting the Smoke Screen: Dynamics of Mail Order Bride Migration from the Philippines. Unpublished Ph.D. dissertation. Institute of Social Studies: The Hague. Holland.

De Stoop, C. (1994). Exotic Brides: Herr Schlegal Offers Girls on a Trial Basis. In De Stoop C. (Eds.), *They Are so Sweet Sir: The Cruel World of Traffickers in Filipinas and Other Women* (201-217). Belgium: Limitless Asia.

Ehrenreich, B., and Hochschild, A. R. eds., *Global Women—Nannies, Maids and Sex Workers in the New Economy*. London: Granta Books, 2002.

ESCAP. (1999). *The Impact of Globalization on Population Change and Poverty on Rural Areas*. Asian Population Studies Series 154. United Nations Publication.

Glick Schiller, N., Basch, L., Blanc-Szanton, C. (1995). From Immigrant to Transmigrant: Theorizing Transnational Migration. *Anthropological Quarterly* 68 (1), 48-63.

Glodava, M., & Onizuka. R. (1994). *Mail-Order Brides: Women for Sale*. Fort Collins, Colo: Alaken.

Guarniza, L. E. (2003). The Economics of Transnational Living. *International Migration Review* 37 (3), 666-699.

Hondagneu-Sotelo, P. (2001). *Doméstica: Immigrant Workers Cleaning and Caring in the Shadows of Affluence*. Berkeley: University of California Press.

Johnson, E. (1999). *Alternative Access—Mail-Order Brides on the Internet: A Study of Russian Women in Kyrgyzstan*. Manchester: Visions and Voices Conference.

Kojima, Y. (2001). In the Business of Cultural Reproduction: Theoretical Implications of the Mail Order Bride Phenomenon. *Women's Studies International Forum*, 24 (2), 199-210.

Light, I. & Bhachu, P. (Eds.). (1993). *Immigration and Entrepreneurship—Culture, Capital, and Ethnic Networks*. New Brunswick and London: Transaction Publishers.

Lisborg, A. (2001). *Fra moderne slaver til modige entreprenører: Om prostitutions relateret migration fra Thailand til Danmark. Kvinder, Køn & Forskning*, 3 (01).

LOKK. (2003). *Når drømme og håb forvandles til mareridt: En rapport om danske mænds vold mod udenlandske kvinder og børn* ("When dreams and hopes turn into a nightmare: The violence of Danish men against women and children from foreign countries"). Funded by the Danish Ministry for Refugees, Immigrants and Integration & OAK Foundation.

Makow, H. A *Long Way to go for a Date*. Silas Green, 2000.

Massey, D. S. (1988). Economic Development and International Migration in a Comparative Perspective. *Population and Development Review* 14, 383-413.

Moustgaard, U., & Brun, H. *Kroppe over grænser—Når kvinder handles til Danmark*. Copenhagen: Informations Forlag, 2001.

Parreñas, R. S. *Servants of Globalization—Women, Migration and Domestic work*. Stanford University Press, 2001.

Pettman, J. J. An International Political Economy of Sex. In Kofman and Young, eds., *Globalization: Theory and Practice*. Pinter, 1996.

Sørensen, N. N.(2003). *Den globale hjertetransplantation*. Downloaded 10 September 2003 at www.kvinfo.dk/FORUM.

Sassen, S. (2002). Countergeographies of Globalization—The Feminization of Survival. Paper presented at the conference Gender Budgets, Financial Markets, Financing for Development. Berlin: Heinrich-Boell Foundation. 19th-20th February 2002.

Schaeffer-Grabiel, F. (2004). Cyberbrides and Global Imaginaries: Mexican Women's Turn from the National to the Foreign. *Space & Culture* 7 (1):33-48.

Viborg Amt. (2003) *Indvandrere og efterkommere* (Immigrants and their descendants) Viborg Amt.

Four

BEYOND TRAFFICKING, AGENCY AND RIGHTS:
A CAPABILITIES PERSPECTIVE ON FILIPINA EXPERIENCES
OF DOMESTIC WORK IN PARIS AND HONG KONG

Leah Briones

Abstract

Current analyses of trafficking in unskilled female migrant labor are dominated by
the concepts of victimization, agency and rights. So far, however, such concepts have
done more to legitimate receiving countries' border control protection than to protect
the livelihood needs of these migrant workers. Drawing on the experiences of Filipina
domestic workers in Paris and Hong Kong, this paper uses Nussbaum's Capabilities
Approach to question the efficacy of the current anti-trafficking discourse

Introduction

Traditionally, international anti-trafficking policies have concentrated on the protection
of women trafficked, within prostitution. In recent decades, there has been much
reported and published on the noticeable increase of the number of women from
poor areas of the world who migrate to rich countries for domestic work, and their
exploitation by employers and traffickers. In 2000, the UN Trafficking Protocol also
recognized overseas domestic workers (ODWs) as unskilled female labor migrants
vulnerable to slavery and similar practices.[1] Despite this wider knowledge base, the
anti-trafficking principle of "rescuing, reintegrating and repatriating" the victim,
continues to persist. Far from protecting the migrant worker and her livelihood needs,
this victim-based approach continues to result instead in legitimizing more protection
for receiving countries' borders (for example, Doezema, 2000; 2002). An emerging
perspective underscoring migrant women's agency is producing a counter-approach
that fights for ODWs' rights: not as victims, but as workers. These efforts, however,
remain hampered by increasing inequality within the global economy and tightening
immigration policies. From poor countries with very limited livelihood options, these

migrant women choose overseas domestic work, often at the expense of their human rights. As migrants, they are outsiders whose rights are superseded by the rights of the sovereign, receiving-state, while unenforceable by the sending state (Stasiulis and Bakan, 1997). Consequently, the current rights approach has done little to change the historical course of anti-trafficking policy.

This paper employs Nussbaum's Capabilities Approach to tackle the limitations of the rights-based approach in responding to the situation of migrant domestic workers. Focusing on women domestic workers migrating from the Philippines, the paper shows how current polarized analyses of ODWs theoretically conflate agency with rights, and practically remain aloof to their subjects' needs for sustainable livelihoods. It then draws from Filipina experiences of domestic work in Paris and Hong Kong[2] to show how it is the question of capability (what she is actually able to do and be) rather than rights (what she is entitled to do and be) with which the ODW is most immediately concerned. I then use the Capabilities Approach to theorize agency with rights, and to conclude that rights-based initiatives should foreground capability as the political goal. The current challenges faced by both the victim and agency-based approaches show that unless the ODW's agency is conceptualised in terms of its capability to be practiced, it will continue to provide little impact on the progress of current policy actions on who to protect—the Slave or the Worker; and what to protect—rights or livelihoods.

Constrained Agency and the Problem of Rights

Since the 1970s, women in the Philippines have faced increasing unemployment and insufficient wages. Thus, many have resorted to participating in the global labor market for domestic work. More recently, Filipina overseas domestic workers (FODWs) have come to form the majority of female labor migration from the Philippines, which accounts for around 70% of the country's international labor migrants (POEA 2005). While their participation allows access to wages that sustain livelihood expenses, ranging from raising capital for micro-enterprises to raising families, it remains fraught with violations of their human rights. Given this contradictory situation, studies of FODWs have portrayed them as either coerced or oppressed victims/slaves, or as consenting and empowered agents/workers. Feminists arguing for "the victim" attribute the increase in poor women's migration for work to the expansion of a patriarchal, capitalist global political economy (see especially Ehrenreich and Hochschild, 2002; Sassen, 1988; 1998; 2002a; 2002b). They argue that the structural gendered inequality in the global economy is manifested in both the labor emigration policies of sending countries and the immigration and domestic labor employment policies of receiving countries, which devalue and render migrant women workers invisible. They describe (ODWs) as export-import traded commodities whose labor is reduced and confined to slave-like servitude within the domestic work sector of receiving countries (Aguilar and Lacsamana, 2004; Altink, 1995; Anderson, 2000; Bakan & Stasiulis, 1997; Bals, 1999;

Chang, 2000; Cheng, 1996; Chin, 1998; Constable, 1997; Ehrenreich and Hochschild, 2002; Heyzer, Nijeholt, and Weerakoon, 1994; Li, Findlay, and Jones, 1998; Lindio-McGovern, 2003; Rhacel S. Parreñas, 2000; 2001; Pratt, 1997; D Stasiulis and Bakan, 1996; 1997; 2000). Supporting these observations are human rights-based NGOs findings on ODW abuse worldwide, which includes the withholding of wages/passports, near or total confinement in employers' homes, physical and sexual harm as well as psychological abuse, in terms of constant threats of violence (e.g. Social Alert, 2000). In contrast, some feminist works employ the concept of "agency" to highlight the more positive aspects of FODW experiences. These agency-centered studies highlight the individual migrant's decisions to pursue livelihood opportunities in the global labor market, and foreground the migrant's social and financial capital gains from international labor migration (Barber, 2000; Ebron, 2002; Ford, 2001; Gibson, Law, and McKay, 2001; Liane Mozère, 2001; Tacoli, 1999). These studies draw on the increasing acknowledgment in migration studies that international labor migration can empower poor migrant women by enabling the formation of trans-national households, which in turn alter gender power-relations back in their own households to favor the migrant woman (Hondagneu-Sotelo, 1994; Morokvasic, 1984). In addition, international labor migration can politically empower migrant women to participate in collective resistance through migrant networks (Yamanaka & Piper, 2003 pp. 1-2).

Policy actions remain divided along the same lines. The feminist-structuralist works and human rights NGOs findings on domestic slavery, for example, have resulted in a "modern slavery" discourse which has enabled some NGOs to successfully lobby for the "protection" of victims under anti-trafficking laws (see for example the NGOs mentioned in the policy reports by the Council of Europe on domestic slavery, 2001; 2004). In contrast, there are those who call for a paradigm shift in policy approaches from the protection of the victim, to the assertion of their rights. Schwenken (2003, 2005), for instance, uses the case of RESPECT, a Europe-wide network of ODWs and their supporters, to demonstrate that viewing ODWs as women with voice and agency, rather than as passive victims, allows the rights of ODWs to be heard and respected, rather than repressed, by the receiving state. The RESPECT network calls for the rights of ODWs for mobility both within the states of the European Union (EU) and the EU itself, as well as the right to earn their livelihoods by being recognized as valuable workers doing "proper work." Schwenken argues that recognizing the domestic worker as a bearer of political rights provides the platform from which a political imperative for foregrounding the agency of ODWs can be achieved.

This polarized approach to ODWs shares much in common with the debate over prostitution in less-developed countries, and more recently, over trafficking in sex from less-developed countries, within feminism. Kempadoo (1999) and Agustìn (2005), for instance, note the tensions between advocates of "the victim" who emphasize aspects of violence and sexual slavery in prostitution, and advocates of "the agent" who propose prostitution as "work" for women who have limited livelihood options. Doezema (2000; 2002) further shows how the debate extends to the issue of the victim's "coercion" versus the agent's "consent" in international policies against human trafficking. She traces the debate back to western feminist abolitionists in the early twentieth century who, under the banner of human rights, called for protection of the female victim from trafficking and other forms of slavery. However, Doezema argues that such policies result in justifying repressive measures that deny prostitutes of their autonomy and agency, while restricting their mobility to cross international borders in search of work. Indeed, there has been mounting criticism against the current protective measures that focus more on receiving-countries' concerns of border control rather than on securing sustainable livelihoods for ODWs (Agustìn, 2005; Anderson and Davidson, 2003, p. 55; Limanowska, 2004; Pécoud and de Guchteneire, 2005, p. 3; Piper, 2005; van den Anker, 2004, pp. 3-4).

Much like the state of the debate on "prostitution," the growing case for ODWs' agency and the assertive claim to rights entailed stops short of addressing the root cause of migrants' needs for sustainable livelihoods. At the conceptual level, the idea of agency seems to be conflated with rights. It is not clear how having agency directly leads to having rights. Indeed, what type of agency is being conflated with what type of rights? In the particular issue of livelihoods for FODWs, for example, can a FODW earn a livelihood by being a slave? Is she therefore practicing a type of agency without rights? Or is she using her agency to practice her right to earn a livelihood over her right to non-enslavement?

These difficulties with the concept of agency become apparent when considering the feasibility of the rights-based approach in the political arena. Firstly, the focus on rights is concerned with the domestic labor laws and related immigration rules within the borders of the receiving states. This ignores those who undertake circular migration, or who are yet to enter receiving countries' borders, or to return to their country of origin. As Cox (1997) and Sim (2002) have identified, the vulnerability of ODWs extends beyond the workplace destination, and occurs as a process that begins from preparation and recruitment for going abroad, to working abroad, but also to returning home. Secondly, because the focus on rights is based on the demand of overseas domestic work, the supply side, bound in underdevelopment and lack of livelihood access in countries of origin, does not receive appropriate attention. This leads to the third problem in agency-based analysis; that is, the failure to incorporate the role of broader structural contexts that push and facilitate the movements of ODWs through multiple borders, and in the case of circular migration, multiple times. The fourth problem pertains to the applicability of rights in host settings, as well as in the international political arena. In host settings, the issue of rights is in itself precarious and is received differently. For example, while ODWs' rights in western European receiving countries are attached to the right to citizenship, ODWs' rights in receiving countries in Asia are limited to short-term contracts (Battistella, 2002; Bell and Piper, 2005). Internationally, the fight for rights seems futile in the face of a lack of political will, by both sending and receiving states. The 1990 United Nations Convention on the Rights of

All Migrants and their Families remains unratified by receiving countries. Where it has been ratified by the sending country, limited financial and technical capacity to enforce the rules of the Convention, has resulted in a rights-based approach that is practically ineffective (Pécoud and de Guchteneire, 2004, pp. 12-17). Last, a rights-based approach fails to consider the impact of increased rights on the sustainability of livelihoods, even within borders. More rights could lead to demands for better wages and working conditions, and probably citizenship. In turn, this could lead to receiving states closing off the migrant domestic labor market since pressure on state resources would make it preferable to encourage citizens to undertake the work instead. After all, the reason ODWs are "imported" (and tolerated, if illegal) in the first place is because they are cheap, flexible, and expendable. Conversely, increased rights can speed up the process of saturation of the overseas domestic work labor market, as supply from the poor and populous countries rapidly expands. In both cases, the issue of sustainable livelihoods for migrant workers could become even more precarious as employment opportunities contract. In many senses, having rights is not necessarily conducive to the practice of agency when the agent is in such highly constraining circumstances.

Data and Method

As part of a study on the nature of constraints to FODW agency, I conducted fieldwork in Paris and Hong Kong to interview twenty-four FODWs (twelve in each city).[3] Paris and Hong Kong were chosen as research sites because of their disparate conditions; Paris as a site for undocumented migrant work, and Hong Kong for documented (the majority of FODWs in Paris are undocumented while the majority in Hong Kong are documented).[4] Comparatively, the study sought to determine to what degree the FODW's inclusion as either documented or undocumented worker entitles her to citizenship and other rights-based claims. The study also sought to learn from individual migrants' experiences of documented and undocumented status, within national settings. To fully account for the issues of constraints to FODW agency, the sample in each city consisted one-third of those who had experienced enslavement; another third, of those who were oppressed and/or abused (in ways that the respondents' considered different from enslavement); and the last third, of those who enjoyed satisfactory working and living conditions and who saw their situations as similar to other wageworkers in gainful employment. Because the criteria for determining who is enslaved, oppressed/abused or contentedly employed rested on the FODWs' own classification of the situation, variations to the three categories were created (see Table 1).[5] In this paper, I focus on the life trajectories of JB and Ellen to provide some insights into the complex and temporally fluid relationship between their agency and the constraints they face as ODWs. JB is a recently turned documented worker in Paris who has always seen her situation as that of a "Wageworker," while Ellen is a documented worker in Hong Kong who classified her situation as that of a "Slave Wageworker."

Table 1. FODWs' classifications of their work situation in Paris and Hong Kong

FODWs in Paris	Own Classification
Delia	Wageworker
Felise	Wageworker
Gudilia	Wageworker
Mila	Wageworker
Nene	Wageworker
Indiana	Wageworker
JB	Wageworker
Minda	Former Slave now Wageworker
Melanie	Former Slave now Wageworker
Sally	Former Slave now Wageworker
Helena	Former Slave now Abused Wageworker
Lani	Former Slave now Wageworker
FODWs in HK	Own Classification
Michelle	Wageworker
Red	Wageworker
Virgo	Wageworker
Bernie	Wageworker
Loveley	Wageworker
Lilia	Wageworker
Ellen	Slave Wageworker
Jinky	Abused Wageworker
Alili	Oppressed Wageworker
Amity	Oppressed/Abused Wageworker
Gemini	Slave
Ana	Slave

Immigration Control and Migrant Domestic Labor Policy in France and Hong Kong

Increasing inequality between developed and developing countries is a major contributing factor to the rapid growth of irregular migration (for example, Massey and Taylor, 2006; Stalker, 2000). A main consequence of this inequality has been the growth of demands for services in developed economies, from developing economies. Feminist geographers point to the sexual and racial division of labor in the international labor market that underlies this supply-demand nexus. They argue that the division of labor places unskilled migrant women work at the lowest end of production and for the lowest pay, in the feminized jobs of domestic and sex work (De Dios, 1992; Glenn, 1992; Lee, 1996; Mies, 1998; Sassen, 1984). This has produced what Sassen (2002a) has termed "global cities and survival circuits"; poor women go to work for high-paid workers in global cities, and survival circuits are composed of migrant networks that facilitate recruitment, sometimes involving precarious dealings with smugglers and traffickers to ensure employment. Paris and Hong Kong are such global cities in which many low-income women from developing countries come to work. During 1996, an estimated 17000 FODWs were in France (Anderson, 1996; Torrés, 1996), with a significant number based in Paris.[6] Hong Kong, through a bi-lateral ODWs labor-importation scheme, hosts around 220 000 FODWs (HKID, 2005). Despite rising demand in both France and Hong Kong, state immigration and domestic labor employment policies largely leave unrecognized the crucial contribution of ODWs to national growth, as well as to the national well-being of households (Anderson, 2000; Constable, 1997; Narula, 1999; Tam, 1999).

French immigration policies do not acknowledge independent female entry, forcing many female migrant workers to enter France through tourist visas which most overstay, or by using the services of smugglers and/or traffickers (Misra, Woodring, and Merz, 2005). Some arrive as escapees from the relatively harsh working and living conditions in the Middle East, or from Middle Eastern employers who have settled in France, or who go to France for their vacation. Once in the country, the migrant women are able to remain hidden from immigration authorities by engaging in "invisible" employment such as domestic work. Although France has among the most responsive labor regulations governing domestic work (Blackett, 1998; Cabral, 2001), these regulations apply only to those who are legally employed. The regulations do not address the need to issue work permits for domestic workers, leaving the status of legal employment to the discretion of the employer. However, few employers register their employees, further ensuring that exploitation in relation to their working conditions, pay, and social benefits remains largely hidden (Narula, 1999, p. 161). Similarly, a government initiative requiring employers to legalize their domestic workers, remains largely ineffective as many employers continue to employ cheap and flexible labor, which if documented, would mean higher wages and taxes, and ultimately less control over their employees (see for example, Mozère, Maury, Fijalkow, Dahan, and Lenhart, 2001). In Hong Kong, the Administration's strictly regulated ODW sector provides a set minimum wage, a formal labor contract, which is contestable in its labor courts, and an Ordinance that provides for the rights of migrant workers to join/form trade unions. However, ODWs remain on-call for 24 hours, as contracts do not specify working hours. The contract is also bound to immigration policies that limit ODWs to two-year terms, to deter any claims to citizenship.[7] In 1987, the Administration introduced the Two Week rule,[8] in response to a perceived increase in irregular activities by ODWs. It requires ODWs to leave its borders within two weeks of the termination of their contracts. This means that any labor conflict with employers has a strong likelihood of leading to deportation, and therefore loss of employment for the ODW. Thus, as in France, Hong Kong state policies push ODWs into an invisible realm, in which ODWs stand powerless against (potentially) abusive employers.[9]

In addition to employer-inflicted abuse, NGOs in France and Hong Kong have revealed how practices by recruitment agents/agencies can drive ODWs into slave-like conditions. These practices can range from extortionate rates charged by the agents/agencies that lead to debt-bondage to collusion with employers and/or smugglers and traffickers. Globally, NGOs have been able to broaden their influence at regional and international levels by forming transnational activist networks that fight for domestic workers' rights around the world. The most active NGOs compose mainly of migrant workers, both documented and undocumented (see for example, Law, 2002; Stasiulis and Bakan, 1997). This points to an important characteristic of ODW migration which has received little attention in the literature: that of tenacity. Even in documented situations such as Hong Kong, this observation holds true for the many who stay there (by renewing contracts or, in the minority of cases, by successfully circumventing state rules) for as long as possible. Further evidence to this tenacious migration is the shift in NGO services which used to deal with repatriation but now concentrates on livelihood support (see for example, Roberts in Ball and Piper, 2002, p. 1030). Thus, despite oppressive state policies, significant numbers of FODWs have remained in France and Hong Kong.

Given such structural constraints on the one hand, and their persistent high numbers and growing activism for the right to work and stay in destination countries on the other, FODW participation in overseas domestic work cannot be explained only by structural forces of the global labor market, nor can it be explained through analysis of the voluntaristic orientations of the individual migrants. Such analysis may provide an important basis for understanding how migrants practice agency, but they say little of the migrant's "staying power." Indeed, what are the factors, which determine the migrant's ability to continue in overseas domestic work, and how do they relate with the practice of her highly constrained agency? In other words, what is required to make a victim a victor?[10]

The Issue of Capability: Constraints in the Host Locale

Regardless of self-classifications, legal status and work locations, the respondents' definition of wagework generally reflect the liberal view of the free labor wage contract. In contrast, definitions of enslavement are fluid. While the narratives on slavery are generally reflective of the feminist structuralist perspective that sees slavery and similar practices in contravention to the labor rights attached to wage work, they importantly reveal an intrinsic link between slavery and wagework in the FODW experience. As Ellen in Hong Kong explains:

> [I'm] a "slave wageworker." You see, this is the way I think about my situation:
> abuse, enslavement, whatever—they are those negative things natural to life;
> natural to looking for money. It's a fact that it's hard to find and earn money.

If you don't move or act or do, neither will money fall into your lap. So that although destiny has put me here in domestic work it has likewise put office workers in office work, say. But essentially, it is just work and we still have to work hard for our money. Enslavement is natural to my type of work, so that I can say, I am a slave—but I am not abused. My employers are higher in status but they still give me my pay and look after me when I'm sick. Just like other employers out there.

Ellen demonstrates here not only how wagework and slavery can be inseparably experienced but also philosophically accepted by the FODW. This perspective of "slavery" is implicitly shared across the range of respondents' situations, from those who classified themselves as slaves to those who classified themselves as wageworkers. However, it would seem that slavery is seen as acceptable on the two conditions: that one is remunerated for the work provided, and one is not subjected to violent abuse.[11] Thus, Ellen could endure domestic work with her employers:

In the earlier years of my work . . . there was little food, long hours; sleeping at 1am and waking at 6am. At the time I had to look after a 3-year old child while also cleaning and grocery shopping . . . I was dying of homesickness . . . You need to be very resilient in this job. For example, my employers are very strict on top of the heavy workload. So I just close my eyes to their never-ending demands while just keeping at the work. As [12] years passed, their children grew up and the work became lighter. I began to feel like they didn't need me anymore . . . so I suggested that maybe I should return home for good . . . [But] they still wanted to employ me . . . So this is why I am still with them now.

While much of this account highlights the subordinate position of ODWs in the employer/master—domestic worker/servant relationship, it is important to note that Ellen's central concern is not so much the abuse, or how, why and to what extent it occurs. Rather, she is determined to stay in overseas domestic work. Although Ellen has built her own house in the Philippines and has put away some savings for her retirement, she has decided to continue in overseas domestic work because she wants to help her family in the Philippines:

I have nieces and nephews who are in college. If God could help my body to stay strong, I would like to stay here [for another two years] so that I can help pay for their education until they have finished college. I'm starting to feel tired now . . . I[also] have a nephew who has leukemia and so I help my sister out with his hospital bills.

JB also, having worked undocumented in Paris for five years, plans to stay by "hook or by crook":

> My employers [recently] helped me get my papers . . . others who have been here for 10-12 years still can't get their papers [so] I have to say that the real help came from Heaven.

> But [if challenged] I know that the Filipinas without papers would probably fight for their right to stay [and work here]. You see they don't want to go back to the Philippines. Life is too impossible there. Look at them now, they will just go home for about a month and then they want to come back here again because they've ran out of money there.

> Actually for me, I don't ever want to return home. I will do my best to stay here by hook or by crook. If say, my fight or "crook way" was unsuccessful, then I would return to the Philippines with my savings and start up a business. If that fails, then I would have to go abroad again [to work as an ODW].

Ellen and JB illuminate here that for the FODW, "work" is about getting paid or earning a livelihood, which is intrinsically bound to being in the host locale, where cases of abuse abounds. However, there must be caution in prematurely accepting the constraints presented by employer/host locale-inflicted abuse, as a conclusion of the FODW situation. Ellen and JB tell of the harsh tradeoffs that are necessary to achieve their valued ends of earning a livelihood:

> For me, I really didn't want to leave my family behind . . . going overseas is like taking up a job I really didn't want but it was one that could help my family, so I really had no choice.

> Ellen, Hong Kong

> The Philippines is my [home]. It's where I grew up and it's where my family is . . . The only thing that doesn't make it home is that there is no money to live. How can you enjoy life with your family when you have to worry about the most basic things in life like a safe and clean environment in which the children can grow up, access to good food, education and health services? You can't have a home when you have no money. But if I had money, I tell you, I would definitely stay in the Philippines.

> JB, Paris

As Ellen has earlier put it, such harsh tradeoffs and other constraints are "natural to making money." Given this rather hopeless rationalization of the FODW situation, it is important to underscore the reasons that "shackle" her to the host locale in the first place. These reasons, as explored in the following discussion, arise out of structural constraints that lay outside of, but that have a direct impact on her participation in, the labor market of the host locale.

Beyond the Host Locale: The Primary and Encompassing Constraint

To grasp the more complete nature of constraints to FODW agency, it is important to go back to the beginning of the FODWs' journey as prospective migrants:

> When I graduated from college [in the Visayas[12]] . . . I thought I would go to Manila to find a job. It wasn't easy so I took up a domestic worker job there with a Visayan woman who had a Chinese husband who ran an autosupply shop. I did everything from the cooking, housework and the shop-keeping. One day, a nephew visited from Hong Kong. I was then asked if I wanted to go to Hong Kong. By the time my contract papers came, I really didn't want to go . . . . But at the time . . . my mother had died and my father was put into hospital . . . . I thought to myself "what am I going to do?" I couldn't afford the hospital bills . . . I was only earning around P1000/mth. My siblings were all married and they were struggling with their own financial situations. I felt like I was the one who could really help . . . . so here I am.

> [I am still here because I need to help my family]. They write to me and ask for my help. I know that it's the obligations of the parents themselves to look after themselves and their own children. But I can see that my sisters and brothers are just not able to because they are not earning as much as me . . . You see, in our province, the reality is even though there are some jobs, they earn just enough for their food. If hospital and other unexpected bills come along, what are they to do?

> Ellen, Hong Kong

> I was a Teacher in the Philippines . . . . I was very determined to go abroad [and earn] because I didn't want my family and I to be hungry all our lives. My cousin has a recruitment agency . . . and he found work for me in Thailand . . . as a drummer for a band. But the pay was as lousy as you would get in the Philippines. A friend told me about Paris and arranged my flight and "tourist" visa.

> When I was growing up in our province, I only needed a little to survive. Today, the 300 Euros I remit to my siblings and their family every month is not enough . . . Just this afternoon, I was crying because I was just on the phone with my brother. Again, he was asking for money. I said to him "but I just sent you some money recently." He replied, "oh but the tap broke and so we had to buy a new one." So I had to cry because I work so hard here for my money.

> I have my formal work but I also take on another job over the weekend [undeclared]. In this way, I can earn up to 2000 Euros per month and I don't

have to pay for my board and food. The price you pay for the higher income, however, is that you can't go home because it will be near impossible to get back in here again . . . Those who don't eventually get papers will just have to stay here forever. Anyway, they are looked after here better than they would be in the Philippines. If they should get sick here and need an operation, they don't have to spend a cent, if they can't afford it[13] . . . Come to think of it, it's probably a good thing not to go home. When you go home, you end up dead broke because you spend all your savings! And so we must clean toilets here forever; to keep refilling our pockets! . . . I could even say that my family back home, because I feel so guilty if I don't send them money, "enslaves" me. I wouldn't work two jobs and get so tired if they could look after themselves. But I feel so guilty when I have the latest fashion clothing here and good food, when members of my family do without them.

JB, Wageworker, Paris

Ellen and JB's account of the reasons for why a FODW might "forever" stay in a locale (Paris/Hong Kong) paints a rich picture of what life is like "outside" of the host locale. JB's reflections on the financial decisions behind remaining in Paris on the one hand, and her endurance of working conditions that she sees as akin to enslavement on the other, underscores the structural problems of (under) development in the Philippines. JB underpins the connection between experienced slavery in the host locale and cause of the experience as arising from the locale of origin. As she explains, she works two jobs and gets so tired precisely because her family cannot "live a certain way" without her earnings. Unlike JB, they are in a setting of underdevelopment, and are thus unable to earn enough to buy fashionable clothing and good food. In similar ways, both Ellen's and JB's labor migration illuminates how materialist structural conditions, and the financial and livelihood constraints arising from them, directs their practice of agency. Poverty, in other words, is both the reason and cause for their labor migration (see Campani, 1993, pp. 197-201; Parreñas, 2005, pp. 56-66). Indeed, the great majority of the respondents said they would not have left the Philippines had they been earning enough to support themselves and their families.[14]

Experiences with recruitment agencies are particularly illuminating of the centrality of poverty in the decision to migrate for overseas domestic work. Those who used recruitment agencies had to take out loans from the agencies themselves. Unlike banks, recruitment agencies allow the borrower to loan 100% of funds. Re-payment is then made with the first few months of earned wages, and with extortionately high interest rates. Alternatively, those who cannot raise the recruitment fees or are not willing to take the recruitment agency loan deal, simply cannot go overseas to work. As Ellen tells of her experience:

Although I am here as a direct hire,[15] I've had a brush with a recruiter when I was still in the province. There was a man who came to our province and informed us that for a 20 000 Pesos placement fee, I could go to work in Oman. This was in the late 1980s. I was told I could earn a great deal of money . . . . But my family couldn't raise 20 000 Pesos . . . so I didn't end up going.

In Paris, many who either did not escape from abusive Middle Eastern employers or came directly hired, used the sort of recruitment service that provided "tourist visas" to overstay or the services of smugglers/traffickers. JB had traveled to Paris in the former mode, but as she explains, underlying the many accounts of the dangers of traffickers is the need of FODWs to use them:[16]

Traffickers will always exist in some form as long as there are poor and rich countries. Ultimately, these so-called traffickers can serve as another, more effective form of recruitment for those who would not be allowed in [receiving] countries. [These recruiters] really do end up helping people—because what is life if you are left to starve in the Philippines? Or in other poor countries for that matter.

[I know there are more risks of abuse and enslavement in Hong Kong and the Middle East [than in Paris]]. But . . . let's say, there was no way I could get to Paris, I would still risk Hong Kong and the Middle East because ultimately the risk is a calculated one . . . I would have more chance of living a good life, rather than not at all. It's either these countries or the Philippines.

That poverty is consistently the underlying reasons for FODW migration is important in informing assumptions that most FODWs cannot come from the poorest of the poor since they are "educated" (see for example, Parreñas, 2001). Like the other respondents, Ellen and JB began their labor migration with very limited or insufficient income. Indeed, their experiences remain consistent with reports on the situation of the majority of women in the Philippines that underscore experiences of poverty and high unemployment (e.g. Chant, 1996; Chant & McIlwaine, 1995; Elson, 1991; McCulloch and Stancich, 1998). Furthermore, the very notion of many FODWs being "educated" ignores the politics of education in the Philippines. Having attained educational qualifications in their local provincial regions, JB and Ellen are unfortunately among the many whose college degrees did not come from prestigious universities and are thus unable to secure more gainful employment in the country.

Constraints, Resources and the Issue of Capability to Pursue a Livelihood

Ellen and JB's narratives across Hong Kong and Paris show that their access to resources for the purposes of a livelihood determines their continued participation in overseas domestic work. When considering the livelihood of FODWs, JB and Ellen tell us that it is important to recognize their earning power as not only intrinsically tied to migration for domestic work in the wealthier countries, but also to sustaining life for families back home, including their own upon their return. Olwig and Nyberg-Sorenson (2002) calls this practice of making a living in the context of globalization, "mobile livelihoods." The practice involves the employment of means and strategies to maintain and sustain life in situations of underdevelopment. As Ellen and JB's narratives show, "means" refers to resources in cash and kind accessed through paid domestic work overseas, while "strategies" refer to their engagement with recruiters and other bodies that ensure continued access to resources. In turn, resources are used to reduce poverty and the occurrence of poverty by being refashioned in terms of savings, capital accumulation and investments and/or for daily livelihood expenditures such as food, shelter, medicine and education for themselves and their families.

Of central importance to issues of livelihoods and resources for the FODW is the recognition that they are pursued. This means that if FODW "agency" is exercised, resources simply do not exist for the taking. Rather, they exist in a highly political environment of restrictive immigration controls that constrain FODW use of domestic work migration as a livelihood strategy, but also of underdevelopment processes that have obliterated livelihood resource access in their country of origin. As Ellen and JB highlight, it is underdevelopment in the Philippines and the lack of livelihood resources this entails that can "incapacitate" their agency. Actual access to livelihood resources is therefore an important measure of the capability of FODW agency to be practiced; to make FODW agency effective, we have to look at what she is actually able to do and be. As discussed earlier, the role of rights-based migrant NGOs has been crucial as both a means and strategy to provide continued access to overseas domestic work by opposing immigration and migrant domestic labor policies. However, their inefficacy was also highlighted, pointing in particular to a poor articulation of what rights actually constitute in the case of FODWs, and how they can best be articulated in the context of underdevelopment.

The Value of Nussbaum's Capabilities Approach[17]

Martha Nussbaum's Capabilities Approach (CsA) provides a theoretical framework within which to directly link issues of human rights with FODW agency, and how in turn, they link with livelihood resources. The CsA is a broad and multi-dimensional framework for evaluating individual well-being and the intrinsic experience of development and justice entailed. The CsA argues for a concept of human development to challenge the economic growth-centred orthodox model of measuring development within a country, and thus articulates resources qualitatively rather than quantitatively. Development is seen in "human" terms; in terms of a quality of life and what people are able to do and be, rather than as a measure of how many resources people have or are given by the state. This departure from treating people as factors of production to seeing them instead as agents of production foregrounds the immediacy of capability over functionality. As Nussbaum (2002) puts it, "about a variety of functionings . . . of central importance to a human life, we ask, is the person capable of this or not?" (p. 127). In this way, the CsA finds both theoretical and practical resonance with human rights: capability is seen as a pre-requisite to what a person can actually do and be.

Theoretically, Nussbaum (see especially, 2002; 2005) explains the relationship of capability with human rights through what she terms the "basic," the "internal," and the "combined" aspects of capabilities. Basic capabilities refer to capabilities that are innate to the human condition such as that of practical reason and imagination. Internal capabilities refer to "states of the person herself that are, so far as the person herself is concerned, sufficient conditions for the exercise of the requisite functions." Combined capabilities are "internal capabilities combined with suitable external conditions for the exercise of the function" (2002, p. 132). Through these dimensions of capability, Nussbaum shows how human rights can be understood in two distinct yet integral ways. First, rights can be understood in terms of basic capabilities as "prior to and a ground for the securing of a capability" (2002, p.136). Thus, to take for example, a FODWs' call for a right to a livelihood even when her circumstances obviously do not secure such a right to her, Nussbaum (2002, p. 135) here would argue that, "just in virtue of being human, a [FODW] has a justified claim to have the capability secured to her." Secondly, rights can be understood as equivalent to combined capabilities. In this regard, "to secure a right to a [person] is to put them in a position of capability to go ahead with choosing that function if they should so desire" (2002, p. 135). Because people cannot function without basic capabilities, and cannot function freely as they see fit for their own circumstances without combined capabilities, Nussbaum (2002, p. 131) argues, "capability, not functioning, is the political goal." In this way, capabilities can be seen to provide an informational base that allows tangible and achievable outcomes for the highly abstract and highly contentious notion of human rights. Not only does a CsA define what it means to secure a person's rights, it also ensures the explicit inclusion of the larger structural context involved in securing a person's rights or "combined capabilities." As Nussbaum (2005) asserts, the CsA "makes it clear that securing a right to someone requires making the person really capable of choosing that function . . . [and] makes it clear that all human rights have an economic and material aspect" (p. 175).

In practical terms, Nussbaum has captured the intrinsic relationship between capability and rights by creating a working list of capabilities to ensure that certain capabilities essential to a quality of life are constitutionally secured to the individual. Nussbaum argues for a Capabilities Constitution because the rights approach with particular regard to individuals in the developing world vulnerable to unemployment, hunger, and other resource-challenged situations has proven futile both in theoretical epistemological and practical/enforceable terms. The existing provisions for livelihood, development, economic and social security in various international human rights declarations and conventions are exclusively state-oriented. The very methodology of setting up such conventions are also state-dependent. In contrast, understanding rights as a person's capability transcends the traditional distinction between the private realm of the family and the public sphere within human rights approaches. It also transcends the traditional distinction between state action and state inaction in implementing rights since securing capability in a person will necessarily require state action to provide the economic and material resources necessary to secure that capability.

The articulation of rights in terms of capabilities also serves an important role in providing a basis from which to understand the relationship of agency and capability in the FODW context. Approaching rights from a capability perspective enables a richer appreciation of rights and capabilities as issues of human security rather than human agency i.e. "making the person really capable of choosing that function." A human security paradigm centralises the problems of unequal human development as FODWs experience and respond to it; as a problem rooted, but also structured transnationally by their lives in the host country, as well as back in their homeland. If a Capability Approach "allows comparisons between individuals and across nations as to how well they are doing" (Nussbaum, 2002, p. 122), then as economically disadvantaged individuals from an economically disadvantaged nation, FODWs are not doing so well. They remain deprived of commodities, incomes and other resources, but more specifically, of "combined capabilities." "Educated" Filipinas, for example, share much in common with many educated women in Kerala who cannot find jobs other than sex work in Delhi (Nussbaum 2005, p. 180). The FODWs' standard of living is thus precarious and largely dependent not only on their maintained presence in the host locale, but also on their capability to function or practice their agency within it. In this light, it becomes possible to see that FODW agency requires capability to successfully mediate victimisation; agency in itself is insufficient.

It is a valuable characteristic of the CsA that by exposing the limitations of both "rights" and "agency", it fortifies them with capabilities and capability, respectively. As such, it is able to provide the basis from which a theoretical framework for correcting the conflation of rights with agency is achieved.[18] In both theoretical and practical terms, it illuminates the FODW agency in a more accurate context of FODW capability as the right to access resources in overseas domestic work for the function of sustaining a livelihood. Shifting thus, the FODWs' orientation of her agency from its right to its capability to be practiced, it becomes possible to grasp a more appropriate understanding of FODW agency that questions how far notions of their agency, which differ to the type of policy being promoted, can be imposed on them.

Conclusion: Capability as the Political Goal

The aim of this paper has been to question the current anti-trafficking discourse, using the experiences of a lack of capability of the victims/potential victims of trafficking such as those of FODWs. Although current approaches polarize understanding of the FODW situation in terms of the question "slavery or work?" Filipina experiences of domestic work in Paris and Hong Kong would seem to provide no conclusive evidence to support one or the other. Rather, they show that the issue of gainful work is of central importance to their livelihoods—so much so that they would endure slave-like conditions to keep open the possibility of gainful employment, which, due to the combination of a "push" effect caused by their structural impoverishment in the sending country, and a "pull" by the global economic demand for domestic service, has become available only in overseas domestic work. Given this relationship between slavery/victim and work/agent, as "slaves of their hopes to work," must they choose between work and human rights? (Bals, 1999, p.190). Rather than frame the FODW situation in these dichotomous terms, this paper employed Nussbaum's Capabilities Approach to shift analyses from looking at the lack of choices/rights/agency for (F)ODWs to focusing on their capability to ensure ongoing access to both work and rights. Indeed, as Ellen and JB articulate in this paper, the choice between work and rights should be more accurately viewed as a choice between work (in the host locale) and no work (back in the Philippines).

Taking into consideration the highly constraining environment of overseas domestic work to FODW agency, the paper sought to foreground the central issue of capability to make the issue of protection clearer for both researchers and policymakers: protecting FODW human rights does not guarantee livelihoods, but protecting their livelihood creates the opportunity or capability for securing human rights. Through a Capabilities Approach therefore, it becomes possible to more accurately identify the issue of rights for the FODW as most primarily an issue of capability. However, without completely abandoning the fight for human rights, it is important to consider that the fight be defined in terms of capability. Fighting for capabilities instead of rights can avoid the inherent difficulties in the lack of political will by some states to implement, let alone consider, migrant workers' rights. As Nussbaum (2005: 175) has emphasized, "securing capability in a person will necessarily require state action to secure that capability." Furthermore, and most importantly, framing rights in the context of capability can allow the "victim" herself to reclaim her right for her intended and valued quality of life. So far it is only researchers, state-oriented policymakers and non-ODW based NGOs that have dominated both the discourse and actions on the reclaiming of this right. The practical feasibility of the Capabilities Approach will require further discussion. However, to end here for the moment, in serious recollection of the respondents' struggles to earn a livelihood, is to hopefully mark the beginning of a research and policy agenda that centralizes the issue of capability along with rights for (F)ODW empowerment.

References

Aguilar, D., & Lacsamana, A. (Eds.). (2004). *Women and Globalization*. New York: Humanity Books.

Agustin, L. (2005). Migrants in the Mistress's House: Other Voices in the "Trafficking" Debate. *Social Politics*, 12(1), 96-117.

Altink, S. (1995). *Stolen Lives: Trading Women into Sex and Slavery*. London: Scarlett Press.

Anderson, B. (1996). *Overseas Domestic Workers in the European Union*. Utrecht: Report for Stichting Tegen Vrouwenhandel.

Anderson, B. (2000). *Doing the Dirty Work? The Global Politics of Domestic Labor*. New York: Zed Books.

Anderson, B., & O'Connell Davidson, J. (2003). *Trafficking—A Demand-Led Problem? A Multi-Country Pilot Study*. Sweden: Save the Children.

Bakan, A. B., & Stasiulis, D. K. (Eds.). (1997). *Not One of the Family*. Toronto: University of Toronto Press.

Ball, R., & Piper, N. (2002). Globalisation and Regulation of Citizenship—Filipino Migrant Workers in Japan. *Political Geography*, 21, 1013-1034.

Bals, M. (1999). *Les Domestiques Étrangères Au Canada: Esclaves De L'espoir*. Paris: Logiques sociales éditions de l'Harmattan.

Barber, P. G. (2000). Agency in Philippine Women's Labor Migration and Provisional Diaspora. *Women's Studies International Forum*, 23(4), 399-411.

Battistella, G. (2002). *International Migration in Asia Vis À Vis Europe: An Introduction*. Asian and Pacific Migration Journal, 11(4), 405-414.

Bell, D. A., & Piper, N. (2005). Justice for Migrant Workers? The Case of Foreign Domestic Workers in East Asia. In W. Kymlicka and H. Baogang, eds., *Multiculturalism in Asia* (pp. 196-222). Oxford: Oxford University Press.

Blackett, A. (1998). Making Domestic Work Visible: The Case for Specific Regulation. Geneva: ILO Infocus Programme on Social Dialogue, Labor Law and Labor Administration.

Briones, L. (2006). Beyond Agency and Rights: Capability, Migration and Livelihood in Filipina Experiences of Domestic Work in Paris and Hong Kong. [PhD thesis unpublished] Adelaide, Flinders University, Adelaide.

Campani, G. (1993). Labor Markets and Family Networks: Filipino Women in Italy. In M. Morokvasic and R. Hedwig, eds., *Bridging States and Markets: International Migration in the Early 1990s* (pp. 191-205). Berlin: Sigma.

Chang, K. (2000). Globalization and Its Intimate Others: Filipina Domestic Workers in Hong Kong. In M. H. Marchand and A. S. Runyan, eds., *Gender and Global Restructuring: Sightings, Sites and Resistances* (pp. 27-43). London, New York: Routledge.

Chant, S. (1996). Women's Roles in Recessions and Economic Restructuring in Mexico and the Philippines. *GenEros*, 5(17), 25-38.

Chant, S., & McIlwaine, C. (1995). *Women of a Lesser Cost: Female Labor and Foreign Exchange and Philippine Development*. London: Pluto Press.

Cheng, S. A. (1996). Migrant Women Domestic Workers in Hong Kong, Singapore and Taiwan: A Comparative Analysis. *Asian and Pacific Migration Journal*, 5(1), 139-152.

Chin, C. B. N. (1998). *In Service and Servitude: Foreign Female Domestic Workers and the Malaysian "Modernity" Project*. New York: Columbia University Press.

Constable, N. (1997). *Maid to Order in Hong Kong: Stories of Filipina Workers*. New York: Cornell University Press.

Council of Europe. (2001). *Domestic Slavery: Report to the Parliamentary Assembly*. Strasbourg: Committee on Equal Opportunities for Women and Men.

Council of Europe. (2004). *Domestic Slavery: Servitude, Au Pairs and "Mail-Order Brides."* Strasbourg: Parliamentary Assembly.

Cox, D. (1997). The Vulnerability of Asian Migrant Workers to a Lack of Protection and Violence. *Asian and Pacific Migration Journal*, 6(1), 59-75.

De Dios, A. J. (1992). *Japayukisan*: Filipinas at Risk. In P. Beltran and A. J. De Dios, eds., *Filipino Women Overseas Contract Workers: At What Cost?* Manila: Goodwill Trading Co.

Doezema, J. (2000). Loose Women or Lost Women? The Reemergence of the Myth of White Slavery in Contemporary Discourses of Trafficking in Women. *Gender Issues*, 18(1), 13-54.

Doezema, J. (2002). Who Gets to Choose? Coercion, Consent, and the Un Trafficking Protocol. In R. Masika, ed., *Gender, Trafficking and Slavery* (pp. 20-27). Oxford: Oxfam GB.

Ebron, G. (2002). Not Just the Maid: Negotiating Filipina Indentity in Italy, Intersections: Gender, History and Culture in the Asian Context (pp. Available: www.sshe.murdoch. edu.au/intersections/issue8/ebron.html): no. 8.

Ehrenreich, B., & Hochschild, A. R. (Eds.). (2002). *Global Woman: Nannies, Maids and Sex Workers in the New Economy*. New York: Henry Holt and Company.

Elson, D. (1991). Male Bias in Macro-Economics: The Case of Structural Adjustment. In D. Elson, ed., *Male Bias in the Development Process*. Manchester: Manchester University Press.

Ford, M. (2001). Indonesian Women as Export Commodity: Notes from Tanjung Pinang. *Labor and Management in Development Journal*, 2(5), 2-9.

Gibson, K., Law, L., and McKay, D. (2001). Beyond Heroes and Victims: Filipina Contract Migrants, Economic Activism and Class Transformations. *International Feminist Journal of Politics*, 3(3), 365-386.

Glenn, E. N. (1992). From Servitude to Service Work: Historical Continuities in the Racial Division of Paid Reproductive Labor. *Signs: Journal of Women in Culture and Society*, 18(1), 1-43.

Heyzer, N., G. L. Nijeholt, and N. Weerakoon, eds., (1994). *The Trade in Domestic Workers: Causes, Mechanisms and Consequences of International Migration*. London and New Jersey: Zed Books.

HKID. (2005). Hong Kong Immigration Department, Monthly Statistics for August 2005, Ref: Il/Int/E42561/2005, Hong Kong.

Hondagneu-Sotelo, P. (1994). *Gendered Transitions: Mexican Experiences of Immigration*. Berkeley: University of California Press.

Kempadoo, K. (1999). Slavery or Work? Reconceptualizing Third World Prostitution. *Positions*, 7(1), 225-237.

Law, L. (2002). Sites of Transnational Activism: Filipino Ngos in Hong Kong. In B. Yeoh, P. Teo and S. Huang, eds., *Gender Politics in the Asia Pacific Region* (pp. 205-222). London and New York: Routledge.

Lee, S. M. (1996). Issues in Research on Women, International Migration, and Labor. *Asian and Pacific Migration Journal*, 5(1), 5-26.

Li, F. L. N., A. M. Findlay, and H. Jones. (1998). A Cultural Economy Perspective on Service Sector Migration in the Global City: The Case of Hong Kong. *International Migration*, 36(2), 131-158.

Limanowska, B. (2004). Trafficking in Human Beings in Southeastern Europe. Geneva: joint UNICEF, OSCE-ODIHR and UNOHCHR report.

Lindio-McGovern, L. (2003). Labor Export in the Context of Globalisation: The Experience of Filipino Domestic Workers in Rome. *International Sociology*, 18(3), 513-534.

Massey, D., and J. E. Taylor, J. E., eds. (2006). *International Migration: Prospects and Policies in a Global Market*. Oxford: Oxford University Press.

McCulloch, L., & Stancich, L. (1998). Women and (in)Security: The Case of the Philippines. *Pacific Review*, 11(3), 16-43.

Mies, M. (1998). *Patriarchy and Accumulation on a World Scale: Women in the International Division of Labor*. London: Zed Books.

Misra, J., Woodring, J., & Merz, S. (2005). The Globalization of Carework: Immigration, Economic Restructuring, and the World System. Paper presented at the Paper presented at the 'International Conference on Migration and Domestic Work in *Global Perspective*, Wassenar, Amsterdam, May 26-29.

Momsen, J. H. (1999). Victim or Victor? In J. Henshall Momsen, ed. *Gender, Migration and Domestic Service* (pp. 1-20). London and New York: Routledge.

Morokvasic, M. (1984). *Migrant Women in Europe: A Comparative Perspective*. Paris: UNESCO.

Mozère, L. (2001). *La Philippine Ou La "Mercédès Benz" Des Domestiques. Entre Archaïsme Et Mondialisation. Carrières De Femmes Dans L'informalité.* Sextant(15-16), 297-317.

Mozère, L., Maury, H., Fijalkow, Y., Dahan, V., & Lenhart, C. (2001). *Petites Métiers Urbains Au Féminin Ou Comment Échapper À La Précarisation. Migration et Etudes*, Sept-Oct, No. 101, 1-6.

Narula, R. (1999). Cinderella Need Not Apply: A Study of Paid Domestic Work in Paris. In J. Henshall Momsen, eds., *Gender, Migration and Domestic Service* (pp. 148-163). London: Routledge.

Nussbaum, M. (1988). Nature, Functioning and Capability: Aristotle on Political Distribution. Oxford Studies in *Ancient Philosophy* Supplementary Volume, 145-184.

—. (1992). Human Functioning and Social Justice: In Defense of Aristoteliam Essentialism. *Political Theory*, 20(2), 202-246.

—. (1995). Human Capabilities, Female Human Beings. In M. Nussbaum & J. Glover (Eds.), *Women, Culture and Development: A Study of Human Capabilities* (pp. 61-115). Oxford: Clarendon Press.

—. (1998). Public Philosophy and International Feminism. *Ethics*, 108, 762-796.

—. (2000). *Women and Human Development: The Capabilities Approach*. Cambridge: Cambridge University Press.

—. (2002). Capabilities and Human Rights. In P. De Grieff and C. Ciaran, eds., *Global Justice: Transnational Politics* (pp. 117-150). London, Cambridge, Massachusettes: The MIT Press, London.

—. (2003). Capabilities as Fundamental Entitlements: Sen and Social Justice. *Feminist Economics*, 9(2,3), 33-59.

—. (2004). Beyond the Social Contract: Capabilities and Global Justice. *Oxford Development Studies*, 32(1), 3-18.

—. (2005). Women's Bodies: Violence, Security, Capabilities. *Journal of Human Development*, 6(2), 167-183.

—. (2006). *Frontiers of Justice: Disability, Nationality, Species, Membership.* Cambridge: Harvard University Press.

O'dy, S. (2001). *Esclaves En France*. Paris: Albin Michel.

Olwig, K. F., & Nyberg-Sorensen, N. (2002). Mobile Livelihoods: Making a Living in the World. In K. F. Olwig and N. Nyberg-Sorensen, eds., *Work and Migration: Life and Livelihoods in a Globalizing World* (pp. 1-20). London and New York: Routledge.

Parreñas, R. S. (2000). Migrant Filipina Workers and the International Division of Reproductive Labor. *Gender and Society*, 14(4), 560-580.

Parreñas, R. S. (2001). *Servants of Globalisation: Women, Migration and Domestic Work*. California: Stanford University Press.

Parreñas, R. S. (2005). *Children of Global Migration: Transnational Families and Gendered Woes*. Stanford, California: Stanford University Press.

Pécoud, A., and P. de Guchteneire. (2004). Migration, Human Rights and the United Nations: An Investigation into the Low Ratification Record of the Un Migrant Workers Convention. *Global Migration Perspectives* No. 3, Global Commission on International Migration, Geneva.

—. (2005). Migration without Borders: An Investigation into the Free Movement of People. *Global Migration Perspectives* No. 27, Global Commission on International Migration, Geneva.

Piper, N. (2005). A Problem by a Different Name? A Review of Research on Trafficking in South-East Asia and Oceania. In G. Laczko and E. Gozdziak, eds., *Data and Research on Human Trafficking: A Global Survey* (pp. 203-234). Geneva: International Organisation for Migration.

Pratt, G. (1997). From Registered Nurse to Registered Nanny: Discursive Geographies of Filipina Domestic Workers in Vancouver, B.C. *Economic Geography*, 75(3), 215-236.

Sassen, S. (1984). Notes on the Incorporation of Third World Women into Wage Labor through Immigration and Offshore Production. *International Migration Review*, 18(4), 1144-1167.

Sassen, S. (1988). *The Mobility of Labor and Capital: A Study in International Investment and Labor Flow*. Cambridge: Cambridge University Press.

Sassen, S. (1998). *Globalization and Its Discontents: Essays on the Mobility of People and Money*. New York: The New York Press.

Sassen, S. (2002a). Global Cities and Survival Circuits. In B. Ehrenreich and A. R. Hochschild, eds., *Global Woman: Nannies, Maids and Sex Workers* (pp. 254-274). New York: Henry Holt and Company.

—. (2002b). Women's Burden: Countergeographies of Globalization and the Feminization of Survival. *The Nordic Journal of International Law*, 7(2), 231-262.

Schwenken, H. (2003). Respect for All: The Political Self-Organization of Female Migrant Domestic Workers in the European Union. Refuge: *Canada's Periodical on Refugees*, 21(3), 45-52.

Schwenken, H. (2005). "Domestic Slavery" Versus "Workers Rights": Political Mobilizations of Migrant Domestic Workers in the European Union. Working Paper 116, the Center for Comparative Immigration Studies, University of California, San Diego.

Sim, A. (2002). Organising Discontent: Ngos for Southeast Asian Migrant Workers in Hong Kong. Working Paper Series No. 18, Southeast Asia Research Centre, City University of Hong Kong.

Social Alert. (2000). *Invisible Servitude: An in-Depth Study on Domestic Workers in the World—Description and Recommendations for Global Action*. Brussels: Research on Human Rights Series.

Stalker, P. (2000). *Workers without Frontiers: The Impact of Globalization on International Migration*. Colorado: Lynne Rienner.

Stasiulis, D., and A. B. Bakan. (1996). Structural Adjustment, Citizenship and Foreign Domestic Labor: The Canadian Case. In I. Bakker, ed., *Rethinking Restructuring: Gender and Change in Canada*. Toronto: University of Toronto Press.

—. (1997). Regulation and Resistance: Strategies of Migrant Domestic Workers in Canada and Internationally. *Asian and Pacific Migration Journal*, 6(1), 31-57.

—. (2000). Negotiating Citizenship: The Case of Foreign Domestic Workers in Canada (West Indians and Filipinos). In K. Willis and B. Yeoh, eds., *Gender and Migration* (pp. 383-410). Cheltenham, Northhamptom: Edward Elgar.

Tacoli, C. (1999). International Migration and the Restructuring of Gender Asymmetries: Continuity and Change among Filipino Labor Migrants in Rome. *International Migration Review*, XXXIII(3), 658-682.

Tam, V. C. W. (1999). Foreign Domestic Helpers in Hong Kong and Their Role in Childcare Provision. In J. Henshall Momsen, ed., *Gender, Migration and Domestic Service* (pp. 263-276). London: Routledge.

Torrés, D. (1996). *Esclaves*. Paris: Phebus.

van den Anker, C. (2004). Introduction: Combating Contemporary Slavery. In *The Political Economy of New Slavery* (pp. 1-14). New York: Palgraves Macmillan.

Vaz Cabral, G. (2001). *Les Formes Contemporaines D'esclavage Dans Six Pays De L'union Européene: Autriche, Belgique, Espagne, France, Grande-Bretagne, Italie*. Paris: Comité Contre L'Esclavage Modern (CCEM).

Yamanaka, K., & Piper, N. (2003). An Introductory Overview. *Asian and Pacific Migration Journal*, 12(1-2), 1-20.

Five

ANTI-TRAFFICKING CAMPAIGN AND KARAOKE BAR HOSTESSES IN CHINA[1]

Tiantian Zheng

Abstract

This article discusses the adverse effect upon sex workers of China's abolitionist policy that focuses on forced prostitution and launches anti-trafficking campaigns. The argument developed in this paper is based on over twenty months of fieldwork between 1999 and 2002 in Dalian. I will discuss first the karaoke bar industry and China's policy of anti-trafficking campaigns. I will then demonstrate the impact of this policy on hostesses in karaoke bars. I will follow it with an account of how, unlike the government's perception of forced prostitution, hostesses voluntarily choose their profession and actively seek sex work in countries such as Japan and Singapore.

Introduction

The heavy thud of techno-music drums rumbles from the entrance of a karaoke bar. Three tall and beautiful young women dressed in identical red cheongsams bow elegantly to all entering customers and usher them inside the bar. The entryway spills out into an expansive lobby of glossy marble and ceiling-high mirrors. Over a hundred seductively dressed women are gathered on the left side of the lobby. They sit on three rows of benches, like the audience at an invisible performance. In fact, however, they themselves are the ones being observed. A camera installed on the ceiling provides a live feed to monitors installed inside each private room. Customers can select their escorts from the comfort of couches in these suites. Madams will bring these selected escorts to the customers' private rooms for their companions of the night. The stairs leading to the private rooms on upper floors are lined with two teams of waitresses, all of the same height and with the same hair style, dressed in the same dark embroidered mini skirts, their breasts half exposed and their hips scarcely covered. They greet customers in chorus, "Good evening!"

The upper stories are divided into five sections (A, B, C, D, E) of ten karaoke rooms each. A dressing room for hostesses also serves as a hideout during police raids. None of the activities inside the karaoke rooms can be seen from the outside. Each karaoke room is equipped with a complete set of karaoke equipment, including a 29-inch television set that continuously plays excerpts from erotic Western videos. Each karaoke room is provided with an air-conditioner, rosewood furniture, beautiful window drapes, wallpaper, carpeting, magnificent dim ceiling lights, a big couch, and an end table. There is a space between the television and the end table where clients can dance with hostesses. They can dance either to each other's singing or to the dance music chosen from a song booklet. The couch can be unfolded into a bed at the request of clients. Many karaoke rooms have adjunct secret bedrooms separated by a curtain camouflaged in the same texture and color as the wallpaper. This is designed to prevent discovery in case of a police raid.

In the dimly lit karaoke room, an eighteen-year-old hostess was sitting next to her client, singing a song titled "Why Do You Love Other Women Behind my Back?" (*weishenmo ni beizhe wo ai bieren*) in a provocative voice. As she sang, her fingers were nestled in her client's crotch, she fondled him, leaned her whole body over him, and coquettishly asked him, "My husband (*laogong*), why do you make love to other women behind my back?"

These paragraphs describe an upscale karaoke bar, one of the three principal karaoke bars where I conducted my research in the port city of Dalian, in Liaoning Province. In 1984, following the promising results of more liberal economic policies in Shenzhen, Zhuhai, Shantou, and Xiamen, the State Council granted Dalian the status of "special economic zone" (SEZ) in 1984. By the late 1990s, municipal propaganda boasted that Dalian had developed into the "Hong Kong of the North," the "International Transportation Hinge," an "Advanced Industrial Base," a "Modern Environmental City," and the "Center of Finance, Trade, and Tourism in Northeast Asia."[2]

The rapid growth of the city from a fishing village in the nineteenth century to a metropolis with a population of 5 million has made Dalian a magnet for labor migrants.[3] By the year 1998, the most conservative estimate placed the number of the floating population in Dalian at around 300 thousand.[4] Institutional (household registration policy) and social discrimination force the vast majority of these migrants into the lowest rung of the labor market. Migrants commonly work as construction workers, garbage collectors, restaurant waitresses, domestic maids, factory workers, and bar hostesses.

A substantial fraction of female migrants finds employment in Dalian's booming sex industry. Karaoke bars can be found almost every few steps throughout the whole city. Jian Ping, a reporter for the *New Weekly* mgazine,[5] calls the whole city "a gigantic sauna salon or KTV bar."[6] According to one of the city's police chiefs, Dalian is currently home to 4,000 nightclubs, saunas, and KTV bars. This same police chief estimated that, as of 2001, 80 percent of the total population of migrant women works as hostesses in the nightclub industry.[7] The ratio provided by the police chief sounds astounding. He might be exaggerating a little, but his figure suggests that a high percentage of migrant women works as bar hostesses.

China's sex industry emerged in the wake of economic reforms. During the Mao era, prostitutes were sent to labor camps for education. In 1958, the CCP proudly declared to the world that prostitution had been eradicated, and this success was a symbol of China's transformation into a modern nation.[8] Since the economic reform of 1978, the state's more lenient stance has opened the way for the reemergence of nightclubs and other leisure sites. In order to avoid any residual negative connotations left over from the Mao era, nightclubs in the current post-Mao period are referred to as karaoke bars, KTV plazas, or *liange ting* (literally, "singing practice halls"). Visitors to these bars are mainly middle-aged businessmen, male government officials, entrepreneurs, the nouveau riche, policemen, and foreign investors. Clients can partake of the services offered by the hostesses and at the same time cement social ties (*ying chou*) or *guanxi* (literally, relationships) with their business partners or government officials. Hostesses—mainly rural migrant women—play an indispensable role in the rituals of these male-centered worlds of business and politics.[9]

The companions or hostesses are referred to in Chinese as *sanpei xiaojie*, literally young women who accompany men in three ways. This is generally understood to include varying combinations of alcohol consumption, dancing, singing, and sexual services. Generally between the ages of seventeen and twenty-three, these hostesses provide services that typically include drinking, singing, dancing, playing games, flirting, chatting, and caressing. Beyond the standard service package, some hostesses offer sexual services for an additional fee. Their monthly income ranges from the lowest of 6,000 yuan to tens of thousands of yuan. Hostesses first emerged in modest numbers at the end of the 1980s. Their numbers expanded rapidly in the mid-1990s as karaoke bars became favored sites, not just for male recreation, but also for networking between male businessmen and the local political elites.[10] It was roughly estimated that in 1991, more than 800,000 hostesses were involved in sex work.[11] Karaoke bars and the hostesses they employ are controlled and regulated by the state at the same time that they are used by the state and its agents, many of whom comprise the ranks of the karaoke-bar customer base.

Out of the two hundred hostesses I worked with, only four were natives of Dalian. Most of the others came from rural villages in other parts of China, mainly from the northeast. During my research, I encountered several laid-off urban female workers who were married and in their thirties. It did not take them long to realize that they had entered a market too competitive for them. The younger rural women were much more favored by the clients. Seldom chosen by the clients, the urban laid-off women eventually disappeared. Rural migrant hostesses were extremely averse to exposing their rural origins. At the beginning of my field research, they reported that they were from large metropolitan cities, such as Dalian, Shanghai, and Anshan. It was only after we had become close friends that they confided to me that actually, they were from rural areas on the outskirts of these cities.

Erotic services take place in various establishments that include karaoke bars, hotels, saunas, hair salons, disco and other dance halls, small roadside restaurants, parks, movie houses, and video rooms. Among these establishments, karaoke bars demand the most stringent criteria for the women's height, facial beauty, figure, and such social skills as singing, dancing, flirting, drinking, and conversation. Unlike what is provided by many other establishments, where only intercourse is offered, karaoke-bar hostesses' services are far more encompassing. Only a few of the karaoke-bar hostesses would accept strangers' request for intercourse, for which they charge twice as much as is charged in many other environments except for a few five-star hotels targeted at Japanese clients. Because only the beautiful and skilled can be chosen as company for the night, numerous young women could not survive in the karaoke bar and skidded to other places, such as sauna salons.

Karaoke-bar hostesses often expressed their contempt of women in other establishments whose work involves nothing but sex. At one time, when all sauna bars were closed in Dalian because of a local water shortage, sauna hostesses flocked to karaoke bars. The hostesses commented to each other in low voices, "Look at their gray faces! It's from daily sex work [*dapao*]." Sauna hostesses told me that they could not compete with the karaoke hostesses because "here clients are too particular about your looks and figure. It's different from sauna bars. In sauna bars, appearance is not that important because clients' goal is simply to have sex [*dapao*]." Karaoke-bar hostesses are aware of this difference. They rate their own status second only to foreign hostesses (French and Russian) in renowned hotels.

This chapter unfolds in five parts. First, I discuss my fieldwork in Dalian. Second, I focus on the reasons for hostesses' entry into karaoke bars. Third, I contextualize hostesses' lived experiences in the material and power structures of the karaoke-bar sex industry. Fourth, I discuss hostesses' subjective understandings of sex work. In the last section, I conclude the chapter by exploring hostesses' future plans and aspirations.

Fieldwork

The argument developed in this paper is based on some twenty months of fieldwork, between 1999 and 2002, in Dalian. My research sample includes approximately two hundred bar hostesses in ten karaoke bars. However, I was intensively involved with three karaoke bars in particular, respectively categorized as high, middle, and lower class. The criterion of classification is based on the location of the bar, its organization and management, the level of the hostesses' physical attractiveness, and consumption standards. In this chapter, I mainly focus on the low-level karaoke bar, although I constantly draw on the other two karaoke bars as well. I was introduced to the karaoke bars by a friend who is an official. For a number of reasons, my initial attempt to interact with hostesses was not very successful. They did not have time to listen to me because their eyes were all fixated on each entering client, and they concentrated on the selection process (*shitai*: try the stage). Furthermore, my cultural style marked me as an outsider. They referred to me as "glasses" and "a college student." They ridiculed my student attire, my glasses, and my inability to understand or participate in their sex talk and jokes, and they refused to admit me to their circle. They did not believe in my ability to understand their lives, especially their inner turmoil, simply because I was not "in their shoes." They were also extremely wary of their own security from assaults by the police, hooligans, and others in their dangerous environment. They were also cautious in dealing with each other because any hostess might have some network with VIPs in the city that might harm them. For instance, some hostesses were kept as "spy hostesses" by some local police or officials for self-protection. They might report on other hostesses' prostitution and have these hostesses incarcerated or severely fined. Each hostess therefore used a fake name, a fake hometown, and a fake personal story. To overcome these barriers, I decided to spend more time with the hostesses. I handed in the rooming fees to the bar owner and lived with the hostesses in the karaoke bars. From then on, I was intensely involved in every aspect of their lives. A typical day in the field was as follows. We got up around three o'clock in the afternoon and ordered a light meal from a nearby restaurant. The remainder of the afternoon was free for shopping or visiting the beauty parlor. We ordered dinner at around six o'clock. Around that time, the first customers would begin to trickle into the bar. While waiting to be chosen, we sat in the bar lobby watching video compact disks (VCDs) or television and chatting. Around midnight, we ordered breakfast and went to bed between two and three in the morning.

It was not my initial intention to research hostess-client dynamics by directly servicing clients as a hostess. However, objective circumstances mandated that I wait on clients. My personal profile fits within the range of hostesses' typical characteristics. I am Chinese and female. My fieldwork was conducted when I was twenty-eight and twenty-nine years old, which put me in the "autumn" years of a hostess's career span. This meant that a customer who saw me sitting in the KTV bar lounge would naturally assume that I was a hostess. I was also obliged to minimize the disruption of my research on the bar's normal business operations. According to KTV bar convention, a hostess can legitimately refuse to perform genital or oral sex acts with her customer. Although refusal can and often does spark conflicts between hostesses and clients, these incidents are considered a normal part of business. For a hostess to refuse to wait on a customer, however, is simply unheard of. This meant that if a customer chose me to wait on him, it would have been very difficult for me to refuse.

To avoid clashes with customers, I took certain precautions. I nevertheless became embroiled in several conflicts with customers. This was especially true during my fieldwork in a low-tier bar that is located in Dalian's crime-plagued red light district. Living in the karaoke bars, hostesses and I had to maintain constant vigilance against police raids and attacks by thugs from competing bars in the city (including other bar owners and some frequent clients). At night, three hostesses and I slept on the couches in one of the private rooms rented by customers during operating hours. Every morning before going to sleep, we pushed a couch against the door in case gangsters attempted to break in. At times of danger, we held our breath and turned down the lights, making the room look unoccupied. We escaped danger several times. Experience of common adversity gradually brought us together.

It took the combined efforts of bar owners, bouncers, and hostesses to keep me out of harm's way. I am indebted to them for their advice on safety measures and, at crucial moments, their direct intervention. To extricate me from precarious situations, owners and bouncers incurred the wrath of more than one irate customer, whose outbursts disturbed regular business operations. Hostesses also expended attention and energy that they would have otherwise spent on profit-making matters in order to look after my well-being. Without their sacrifices, my research in the bars would have been too dangerous to continue.

Karaoke Bar Industry and the Anti-Trafficking Campaign

In 1984, the first dance hall appeared in Dalian. It featured a band of six singers and had a capacity of three hundred patrons.[12] It was not until 1988 that the first karaoke bar emerged. Named "Tokyo 898," the bar was financed by a Japanese businessman and run as a Sino-Japanese joint venture. It is said that the bar's karaoke equipment was imported brand-new from Japan—an almost unheard-of extravagance at that time in China's economic development. Customers of the bar included foreign travelers and sailors, government officials, and the nouveaux riches.

After 1988, new karaoke bars mushroomed throughout the city. They became the most fashionable male recreational and commercial activity; closely associated with Western audio and video technology, splendid exterior and interior furnishings, neon lights, high prices, and beautiful hostesses. This drastically different from the previous dance halls, which were organized by work unit, karaoke bars aroused tremendous social curiosity. They suited rich people's desire to experience a "modern" form of consumption, display their vocal talents, and display power and wealth. Patronizing luxurious karaoke bars became a lifestyle, a modern and prestigious symbol often only afforded by such wealthy clients as foreigners, officials, and local nouveaux riche. Blue-collar urban men and migrant workers occasionally visited low-tier karaoke bars to imitate this life style.

Beginning in 1989, with the appearance of karaoke bars, the state has launched periodical nationwide anti-prostitution campaigns to ensure "security and state control." The campaigns are aimed at "cultural purification" and "spiritual civilization." The "erotic company" of hostesses, pornographic television shows, erotic performances, and prostitution within karaoke bars are condemned as "cultural trash" that "destabilize state rule and the socialist system." Restrictions stop short of an outright ban; rather, they intend to bring KTV bars into line with state-defined socialist culture.

China adopts an abolitionist policy that deems prostitution a form of violence against women. Over the past decades, China has published a number of laws to ban prostitution and the third party's involvement in prostitution.[13] This abolitionist policy is predicated upon the belief that no women would choose prostitution voluntarily and that prostitution strips women of their "natural" and legal rights. These series of laws include the first criminal Law in 1979, the 1987 Regulations, the 1984 Criminal Law, the 1991 Decision on Strictly Forbidding the Selling and Buying of Sex, the 1991 Decision on the Severe Punishment of Criminals Who Abduct and Traffic in or Kidnap Women and Children, the 1992 Law on Protecting the Rights and Interests of Women (Women's Law), the Revised Criminal Law of 1997, and the 1999 Entertainment Regulations.

Underlying these laws is the ideology that prostitution humiliates and commodifies women, and that unless prostitution is outlawed, women's position would not be advanced. Because the government holds the belief that women would not choose a profession that violates their own human rights, the purpose of these laws is to prohibit the third party from organizing prostitution, engaging in illicit relations with a prostitute, and trafficking women into prostitution.

The "erotic service" (*seqing peishi*) found in karaoke bars is deemed to go against "socialist spiritual civilization." The exchange of sexual services for money is an "ugly social phenomenon" associated with capitalism and should be wiped out to maintain a healthy socialist cultural environment and "civilized consumption." The main responsibility for administering state policy regarding karaoke bars is divided between the Bureau of Culture (BC) and the Public Security Bureau (PSB). These two agencies respectively represent the government's dual strategy of soft and hard administrative measures. The Bureau of Culture is responsible for ensuring that karaoke bars are managed according to socialist standards of civility and morality. It accomplishes this task through a variety of administrative and regulatory measures. First, BC maintains detailed records on bars' business location, name, proprietor, exterior and interior design, audio and video machines, and other information. Second, strict approval procedures were introduced to reduce the number of karaoke bars. Third, bar owners are required to attend monthly classes organized by the Bureau of Culture to study state policy and law. Those achieving high test-scores are awarded "Civilized Karaoke Bar" plaques that can be displayed inside their bars.[14] Fourth, karaoke bars should have "Chinese" and socialist characteristics. In particular, they should provide mainland Mandarin songs, "healthy and inspiring" revolutionary songs, Chinese-style wallpaper, Chinese paintings, Chinese-style bar names, and Chinese food and snacks. Lurking not far behind these regulations is a palpable sense of crisis induced by the idea that Western influences has begun to erode Chinese culture. As a BC official explained to me: "The imported Western culture in China is like an aircraft carrier-high quality, durable and powerful. Chinese culture, however, resembles a small sampan, only able to float a hundred miles. We need to develop a singing-and-dancing business with Chinese characteristics to attack the foreign cultural market in China."

PSB serves as an "Iron Great Wall" (*gangtie changcheng*), providing the muscle behind state policy. The main vehicle for PSB intervention is the antipornography campaign (*saohuang dafei*), itself a part of a wider comprehensive attack on social deviance known as "crackdowns" (*yanda*—literally, to strike severely). These campaigns last for spurts of three months at a time, to be repeated three times a year, strategically centering on important holidays (National Day and Army Day) and events (the APEC conference). Crackdowns target a potpourri of social ills, ranging from unlicensed video game arcades (said to corrupt the minds of youth), to undocumented rural migrants (said to disrupt urban management).

The combination of prostitution and pornography is a mainstay in the list of crackdown targets. It covers pornographic media (magazines, laser discs) and performances (striptease). The behavior that receives the most organizational resources and labor, however, is the "erotic services" conducted in KTV bars and other commercial establishments (saunas and hair salons). PSB employs a complex system of raids to attack karaoke bars. The techniques are self-described as "guerrilla warfare" (*da youji*), in reference to the heroic efforts of the Communist revolutionaries against the Japanese invaders and nationalists. Raids are divided into several types: "regular raids and shock raids, timed raids and random raids, systematic raids and block raids, daytime raids and night raids." Those PSB units and individuals that perform well—measured in the number of arrested hostesses and amount of fines levied—receive high honors and cash bonuses from their municipal government.

Impact on Hostesses

Local Officials: State policy is problematically translated into reality. The complex interactions between sex industry participants on the one hand and state agents on the other lead to a gap between the "theory" of policy and the "practice" of enforcement. State policy is distorted and even derailed by the self-seeking behavior of local officials. Karaoke bars are an important source of extralegal income. As one PSB official candidly remarked, "Karaoke bars and hostesses are our sources of livelihood. We basically cannot live without them." Because these officials have the arbitrary power to arrest and fine the hostesses, hostesses are extremely apprehensive when they are chosen by an official. In such instances, they must obey the officials' demands including sexual services.

Officials extract economic benefits from karaoke bars through a combination of bribes and fines. State policy is hijacked in the service of officials' personal economic interests, but local officials' exploitation of hostesses are not limited to economic benefits. PSB officials maintain a group of "spy hostesses" (xiaojie jianxi) who report on bar conditions as well as acting as these officials' personal harem. In exchange for their services, hostesses gain immunity from police sanctions. Hostesses allow corrupt officials to get rich, contribute to regional economic development, and enhance officials' political career advancement. There seems to be substantial pressures that push local government into tolerating if not absolutely embracing the karaoke-bar sex industry. I was told that a leader of a sub-region had turned the area into what became heralded as the "largest pornographic sub-region in the province." He built an extravagant mansion and hired hostesses to entertain visiting officials. His "brilliant achievements" eventually satisfied his superiors and gained him high awards, reputation, and promotion.

Bar Owners: While local officials are manipulating state policy to exploit bar owners and hostesses for their personal gain, bar owners have their own strategies. The owners I worked for improvised creative maneuvers to counter local officials.

The owner of the upscale bar—one of three karaoke bars in which I conducted fieldwork—was a well-known local gangster. His karaoke bar opened in 1998 and since then has been the most prosperous bar in the city of Dalian, housing over a hundred hostesses. I came to this karaoke bar in June of 1999. Just beginning my research, I did not know anything about the anti-prostitution campaign until July 1, the anniversary of the birth of the Communist Party. I went to work in the evening as usual that day. I was very surprised to find that all the hostesses' seats were unoccupied—only two hostesses came to work.[15] Not having the faintest idea what was going on, I was immediately led by the madam to the dressing room upstairs and advised to hide there instead of waiting in the hall downstairs. The madam told us to tell whoever saw us that we were salesladies selling beer here. Only after the madam left did I learn from the hostesses that an anti-prostitution campaign started this month, and that police would be raiding this place at some time tonight. Police raids meant that any hostesses in sight would be taken in and arrested. I was told that once you ended up in the police station, it took thousands of yuan to get out. The other two hostesses were in the same situation as I was—all newcomers and completely ignorant about this event. I was very frightened because I did not have a temporary-resident card, and my passport would definitely get me in trouble.[16] Luckily when a couple of men (policemen wearing civilian clothes) came in and asked us a few questions that night, to my surprise, our answer that we were selling beer worked. Later I learned from the madam that our escape was due to the fact that the owner had paid off these policemen. During the last few days of the campaign months, I was living with another hostess. Every midnight, when we took a taxi home from the bar, she instructed me to bend over and hide under the back seats to avoid being seen by policemen. She told me that during the campaign months, numerous policemen patrolled the streets looking for bar hostesses. In China, hostesses fall into a gray area—although the law does not clearly identify them as either illegal or legal in everyday practice, it is recognized that "hostesses" are "sex workers" who provide illegal erotic services and hence are the major subjects of anti-prostitution campaigns.

The bar owner, furious at the loss of business and local officials' restrictions, asked the madam to summon 130 hostesses to a meeting. He expressed his anger and antagonism toward the "unreasonable people working in the government" and listed his tactics to cope with the state policy. Angry as the bar owner is, he utilized nonconfrontational maneuvers—that is, converting illegal bar hostesses into legal employees through shifts of title, dress, identity, work sections, and so on. Such a strategy not only left him some leverage at this critical point of the political campaign, but also allowed him to impose more severe regulations and discipline on the hostesses, who used to operate in a laissez-faire manner.

According to a city official, 1995 marked a change in relations between hostesses and bar owners, from the contract system to an exploitative system. Before the police crackdown in 1995, hostesses were hired by the hundreds on contracts with bar bosses. According to the contract, hostesses received fees from the customers for their services. In addition, bar owners awarded them a percentage of the customers' bills. This contract system was brought to an end in 1995. To explain this change, we must start in the early 1980s.

With the rise in popularity of karaoke bars in Dalian, a red-light district sprang up in the center of the Zhongshan district. At some time around the end of the 1980s and in the

83

early 1990s, a number of karaoke bars were opened on Stalin Road. By all indications, the scope of business must have been considerable. Hostesses were recruited by the hundreds. Every night they scoured the city's seaport for tourists and brought them back to the bars to engage them in sexual activities. During this period, bars and hostesses prospered.

One morning in 1994, a foreigner was seen running out of the area wearing only his underwear. A group of Chinese men followed him, shouting curses and flourishing clubs high in the air. It was said that the foreigner could not afford the tab for the previous night's sexual encounter. Managing to escape with his life, the foreigner subsequently brought charges against the bar's proprietor for exploiting him. The matter quickly escalated into an international conflict between the two affected embassies. The incident even made front-page headlines in the Hong Kong Gazette (*Ta Kung Pao*) in an article titled, "Dalian Red-Light District on Stalin Road."

Fearing that the image of the socialist regime would be tarnished by the scandal, the CCP Central Committee took immediate action by ordering that the area be cleaned up. After overcoming tremendous difficulties in breaking up patron-client ties between local officials and bar owners, the police finally cracked down in 1995.[17] To erase the global and national memory of the incident, the name of the street was changed from Stalin Road to People's Road.

This extreme police crackdown disrupted the previous system by which the bars operated and brought an end to the contract system and the percentage award from bar owners. Ever since, bar hostesses and owners have been under the strict control of local government. Owners view themselves no longer as dependents but as the saviors of the hostesses because they housed the hostesses for security and offered jobs. Ever since 1995, owners started requiring hostesses to turn in 10 percent of their fees to them.

In the particular upscale karaoke bar where I conducted research during the anti-prostitution campaign, the owner extracted additional profit from the hostesses by charging more for their uniforms than they were actually worth. He also seized this chance to record every hostess' biological data. He asked all the hostesses to hand in their duplicate hometown IDs and Dalian temporary residence cards (TRC). He urged those who had not yet purchased or renewed their TRC to do so quickly. He claimed that he would compile a book with a record of their pictures, names, and photocopied TRCs, through which hostesses would be transformed into formal employees working as waitresses. He also effectively controlled their mobility and behaviors. Prior to the crackdown, hostesses were brought to any karaoke room for selection. After the crackdown, hostesses were grouped in tens and assigned to different sections of the bar (ten karaoke rooms in each section). Instead of standing together in the entrance hall, hostesses now only gathered at their designated sections, waiting to be chosen. Every hostess was required to wear the uniform dress with a name card on her chest, in different colors for different sections. Hostesses had to report to the directors (madams) if they were going outside the bar (*chutai*, to offer sexual services in hotels) with clients. They were ordered to be present at the bar at precisely 7:30 p.m. every day and not leave until 12 a.m. unless they went out with clients. Hostesses coming late or leaving early were fined 600 yuan. They had to request a leave or a night off from the director, a request that, in principle, was not granted. The bar owner also demanded that hostesses' walking and speaking manner and singing skills be trained and disciplined. All these new demands, controls, and restrictions on hostesses were produced at this moment of conflict between bar owners and officials. The bar owner ensured the prosperity of his business by manipulating hostesses and maneuvering ways around state policy.

Local implementation of the state's anti-prostitution policy failed to reach the propagated objective of eliminating prostitution; it only aggravated hostesses' working conditions. Police raids of karaoke-bar hostesses made them legally and socially vulnerable. Hostesses' illegal identity forced them to face an exploitative, risky, and violent working environment. If some clients were to disclose their sexual services to the police, they would be subject to extreme humiliation, arrest, handsome fines, and incarceration. Because of this potentially horrifying outcome, hostesses do not disclose their real identity, and this ruse makes it easier for men to be violent toward them and even to murder them. It was reported that in the city of Shenyang, more than 100 hostesses were murdered in 1999.[18] In Dalian, hostesses' bodies were found murdered on the street, but the police could not identify them.[19] When I accompanied my best hostess friend, Wu, to he hometown, I asked her mother if she was worried about Wu's safety in Dalian. At my question, her mother's face sank with distress and torment. She kept silent for a long time before plucking up the strength to tell me that she had believed that Wu had been murdered in Dalian. She said, "I did not hear from her for three months. She did not call me. I did not have her phone number . . . . I really thought she was murdered. You know, it's so common in Dalian. I always heard the news about hostesses' dead bodies found there. I believed Wu was one of them. I was worried sick. I got so sick that I couldn't get up. I thought I was never going to see her again."

Violence

In the upscale bar, the main task of the security guards in green pseudo-military uniforms is to keep the hostesses from leaving before midnight to ensure that clients pay hostesses' tips, and maintain bar security. Occasionally, a team of security guards rushes upstairs like soldiers to quell fights in the karaoke rooms. The suppression of disturbances itself always involved violence and blood. Unarmed or armed (with beer bottles, knives, and glass), fights between drunken clients and between clients and hostesses are daily occurrences. At times, hostesses come downstairs, crying from their injuries: their legs, arms, and breasts black and blue from the hard pinches of some clients. Some hostesses chose to endure whatever abuse they are subjected to, but some opted to quit and consequently received no tips for the time they had put in. Those who clenched their teeth to see it through with big bright smiles held back their tears and complaints for later, when they sent off the clients and returned to the crowd of idle hostesses.

The low-class bar "Romance Dream" is located in the crime-plagued red-light district. The staff includes three multifunctional waiters (madams/doormen/janitors), two bar managers, approximately twenty-seven hostesses, and a barkeep/security guard (*kan changzi de*). As with the high and medium-level bars, blood ties link the bar proprietor and management into a relatively cohesive group. Each bar on this street has to hire a thug as the barkeep. This barkeep has to be a good fighter, otherwise the bar will be forced to close down as a consequence of harassment by roaming gangsters and thugs who roamed the streets. During my research in the bar, I witnessed numerous bloody fights between the barkeep, Bing, and bar waiters and gangsters, clients, and passers-by. I saw Bing and waiters throw heavy stones and chairs at clients and at some passers-by's heads until blood streamed down their heads onto their faces. The bar owner told me that Bing, after having killed and severely injured many men in previous fights, was once sentenced to death. The bar owner spent a great deal of money to finally get Bing out of prison before hiring him as the bar guard. The mere presence of Bing in the bar kept many gangsters and thugs away. According to the owner, if Bing were not in the bar, it would definitely be a disaster: all of the hostesses would flee in fear, and everything would be plundered by gangsters. She entrusted me to Bing and the bar managers to look to my safety.

Gangsters and other bar owners often came to visit. They were all local. When they saw pretty hostesses, they dragged them upstairs and raped them. When they saw less pretty hostesses, they slapped their faces and beat them up. Hostesses were extremely apprehensive about some of the toughest gangsters and thugs. They would run as fast as they could to escape them. Once I fled along with the other hostesses. We escaped by climbing onto the overpass built over the bars, losing our shoes and cutting our feet in the process. It was a very unpleasant experience. Most of the bar hostesses have been raped one or more times by gangsters. Twice the gangsters came in and started to pull me into a karaoke room. Luckily, they were stopped by Bing and the bar managers, who said, "She is not a hostess here. She is my friend." That assurance saved me from imminent danger, but the lingering fear remained.

To protect themselves, almost all the hostesses were connected with one or two street gangsters to gain protection. When a gangster came in, the hostess who was connected with him or to a thug in his group did not need to escape. My best friend, Wu, did not like the bar bouncer of a neighboring bar, but he favored her strongly. Wu had to develop a relationship with him. She told me, "In my home town, nobody dares to touch me because I have a wide network of friends. It's so different here. Here I don't have anyone. No one cares if I am bullied. He is a thug, and he is local. I have to be good to him. I need someone to turn to when I encounter trouble on this street." When Wu was harassed by someone in a different gangster group or by drunken clients, she would call the barkeep for help. On a couple of occasions, the barkeep, upon Wu's call, led a few gangsters into the bar to beat up the drunken client. Wu also hooked up with a bar owner in the city. She told me that these were the key people she turned to when she needed help. Like Wu, other hostesses were connected with a bar owner, a bouncer, or a skilled street fighter. They frequently joked, "We hostesses are relatives of the underworld."

An Exploitative Environment

Hostesses are expected to encourage customers in their consumption of beer, hard liquor, and snacks to boost bar revenues. Known as the minimum charge, these requirements create an onerous burden for hostesses. Hostesses are held responsible for ensuring that customers' expenditures reach the mandated level. To stimulate customers' consumption, hostesses themselves have to continuously consume, especially alcohol. This problem is especially pronounced in the upper-level bar, where the minimum charge is set at 400 yuan. The bathroom is always full of hostesses vomiting into the toilet before returning to their clients to continue drinking. Because of this daily alcohol overdose, most hostesses not only put on weight (which leads to other self-destructive weight-loss practices), but also develop stomach problems that, in severe cases, result in hospitalization.

Hostesses' Struggle

After a while, hostesses develop ways to cope with this inequity. When clients come to the bar looking for hostesses to go offstage, few hostesses consent. It leaves the outsiders with the false impression that few hostesses in this bar go offstage. In reality, however, almost all of the hostesses do, although behind the scenes, to save the entire tip for themselves. One hostess said, "Why should we earn the money for the bar managers? We have established a settled relationship with our clients. We schedule a time outside of the bar to do it. We keep the money in our own pockets. Who needs them as the mediators? Actually, everyone in our bar goes offstage, but secretly."

The bar managers and owner are stingy not only with the hostesses, but also with their steady clients. Wu told me, "Bar business should rely not only on us, but also on the steady clients. However, the bar managers exploit these clients even harder!" Aware of this situation, on the one hand hostesses face pressure to order more food and drinks in karaoke rooms, and, on the other hand, they secretly establish relationships with clients. As their connections are set up, hostesses request that their clients take them out for dinner. In such cases, they not only earn the tip of 100 yuan, but also help their clients save money from the bar overcharges.

Some hostesses sit on several stages at the same time (*cuantai*). For instance, Wu managed to sit on five stages at one time. She said, "The key is: Do not let yourself be seen by your clients when you are sitting on different stages. Once I heard that five of my steady clients were coming on the same night. I was sitting in the first client's karaoke room until it was time for the other clients to come. Then I said, 'I have been feeling really sick these days. I feel really uncomfortable now. Can you leave now and come back some other time?' He agreed and left, offering me a tip. Then, the other clients came one after another. I went into the second client's karaoke room and said, 'Look, my sister has just arrived here in Dalian with a friend. I really have to go to the train station to pick her up. It will take me about an hour or so. I will be back for sure.' Then I left and went into the third client's karaoke room and said, 'Look, my sister will come over to be a hostess. I need to rent her a room, buy her some clothes and merchandise for everyday use. When she starts working here, she will earn money and return the loan to me. Can you give me some money?' He gave me 200 yuan. See, the tip is already in my hands. 'Thanks so much! I am sorry that I have to leave, but I will definitely be back in about forty-five minutes.' Then I repeated the same story in the other two karaoke rooms and promised to be back in, respectively, forty and thirty minutes. After that, I returned to the first karaoke room and said, 'Sorry I am back so late. Oh, I am feeling so exhausted and sick.' Then I stayed there for a few minutes before asking them to leave. They gave me the tip. Then I returned to the other three karaoke rooms, in turn, and repeated the same story."

Hostesses' Aspirations

In this section, I will illustrate that hostessing is not only a lucrative profession for the hostesses, but also a profession that offers them independence and a sense of self-esteem. Their life experience goes contrary to the state rhetoric of forced prostitution and a need for rehabilitation.

Rural women face limited employment opportunities in the city. First, in post-Mao China, there is a lack of a private sector for jobs. Second, as migrants, they often lack the social connections essential for job searching in the already over-saturated urban labor market. Their ability to find work is further hindered by a discriminatory government policy that denies migrants equal status with urban residents. Among the jobs that are available to rural women, most are in low-paid, labor-intensive industries. Under these circumstances, hostessing is a highly attractive employment option. The attractive features of hostessing are many.

Hostessing holds out the allure of high incomes in the least amount of time. Hostesses typically entertain a customer for one to two hours and earn an average tip of 200 to 400 yuan—the equivalent of, and often more than, other rural migrants' monthly wage and almost half the average monthly wage of an urban worker. Working as a hostess provides rural women access to a wide network of influential male figures in the city's business and political sectors. Hostessing requires a minimal upfront investment. Newly arrived hostesses typically borrow money from other hostesses or friends to purchase the clothing and accessories worn while servicing clients. Because of the high profitability of hostessing, the borrower can typically settle her debt with the earnings from one or two sessions with clients. Thus, rural women who lack economic resources can nonetheless enter the workforce as hostesses.

Migrating to countries such as Japan and Singapore to conduct sex work is a dream for many hostesses. During my research, three hostesses managed to travel to Japan and Singapore as sex workers, and they were the models for many other hostesses. Each of these three hostesses turned in 20,000 yuan and passed the interview before being permitted to go through the visa process. They returned to Dalian after having worked in Japan and Singapore for a year. They expressed that it was their ambition to return to these countries and continue working as sex workers.

Learned Urban Cultural Styles

Karaoke bars, as flourishing new cultural spaces in the city, are the places where rural migrant women can achieve a certain degree of self-esteem through the sense being accepted and desired by the urban men who choose them as companions for the night. The karaoke bar is also the place where these women can find secondary socialization by mingling with urban clients, where they feel "urban and cosmopolitan," both culturally and socially. Hostess Ying migrated to the city, and during the mid-1990s, she worked in a private factory, where she was even named the model worker. Eventually, the factory went bankrupt and closed down. Ying was laid off and left without financial sources. Her women friends took her to a dance hall to accompany men. To make a living, she followed them.

I thought nobody would dance with me because of my low quality (*suzhi*) and rural origin. However, to my surprise, some urban men invited me. A man from the Labor Bureau even liked me a lot. Once, I ran into him on the street, and he asked me to have dinner with him in a restaurant. I refused his love but I did go to the restaurant with him. I was such a foolish cunt (*sha bi*)—I was completely ignorant of a restaurant, let alone of all the eating or talking etiquettes. I was such a foolish cunt, so stupid, you mother fucker. I did not know how to eat or talk. I was a peasant. When had I ever seen a restaurant? You know at that time [during the mid-1990s], nobody in my village had ever been to a restaurant. Very few had even heard about it. As a factory worker, I only earned 400 yuan a month. When on earth had I ever seen this amount of money and the atmosphere of the restaurant? After that event, I was so shocked by my incongruity with the urban people. I started working as a dancing companion. Two months later, I went back home with loads of money, several thousand. At that time it was a lot of money. Nobody had ever seen so much money before. The money I earned meant a lot to everyone.

For Ying, living an urban lifestyle affirms an equal status with urbanites; being chosen by urban clients in karaoke bars confirms her self-worth.

Independence

Hostesses' experience of rape and abandonment in the city teaches them not to be duped by men's romantic words, to embrace independence through hostessing. They commented, "Dalian men try to cheat both our bodies and our emotions. Without spending a cent, they get what they want from us." Hostess Guang served as a domestic maid in an urban family before hostessing. Within two months, she was raped three times by her male employer. Hostess Min worked as a restaurant waitress when she was raped and then abandoned by an urban customer. She said, "Urban men take advantage of us both emotionally and physically. We cannot be too innocent (*tai chunjie*) or devoted; otherwise, we will be tricked, used and abandoned. Only women who are not pure can protect themselves."

Han worked as a hairdresser in the city. She lived with an urban man for three years in his home. During this time, she suffered from all kinds of physical and verbal abuse from his aunt and mother. For instance, they accused her of stealing their jewelry and associated her "thieving habits" with her rural background. All this abuse was targeted at her inferior rural background. Han exerted every effort to endure all this inhumane treatment. However, her urban boyfriend also worried that her rural family would become a bottomless pit, eventually draining all his money. He abruptly abandoned her, saying, "Our social status just doesn't match." Devastated, she believed that she would never find happiness unless she became the social and economic equal of the urbanites. She started working as a hostess. Five years later, she was very successful. She possessed two household registrations—one urban and one rural. She purchased two houses, one in her hometown for her parents and one in Dalian for her siblings. She supported her two younger sisters and a brother through school. She paid for the weddings of her four older brothers and sisters, and so on. She is now married to the financial director of a prestigious hotel chain.

Similarly, another hostess, Hong, broke up with her client boyfriend when he failed to offer her the amount of money she expected. She commented, "I myself can earn 100,000 yuan a month from hostessing. To exchange this for his several thousand yuan—so little money—I have to obey everything he says. Who will do that? He thinks I am fresh from the countryside, so I can easily be cheated. With so little money, he wants me to be his second wife and control me as his possession by tying my arms and legs. That's impossible. I want to earn money for myself and spend it happily as I want. There is no way for me to spend his little money at the price of abiding by whatever he has to say."

If rural origin and cultural inferiority is the root of the hierarchical relationship between rural migrant women and urban men, then hostessing offers an opportunity to escape this subordination. As paid work, hostessing represents an act of defiance against the androgynous urban men who freely exploit the women's bodies and emotions. At the bar, men have to pay a high price to hostesses in exchange for even approaching them. This transaction transformed the situation that existed when migrant women were available to men as free dinner at the men's whim.

Hostessing allows the women to gain an economic profit, and therefore independence from men. In the monetary transaction, hostesses attain a certain equality with the urban men by taking advantage of the men's resources. Having financial resources at their disposal brings the women power and confidence otherwise unavailable. Many hostesses who are married or are kept as second wives sneak out of the house to work. Setting up their own separate account allows them to spend their own money at will and secretly support their natal families. The economic power brought by hostessing earned Han and Hong a great degree of independence and equality in social and gender status in both familial and spousal relationship with urban partners.

Conclusion

In this paper, I discussed how the state's anti-prostitution policy is manipulated and usurped by local officials and bar owners for their own ends, leading to a violent working environment for the hostesses. Working amid such exploitative labor relations, hostesses struggle to reallocate male clients' socioeconomic resources into their own hands and subvert the urban-rural hierarchy. Far from the state rhetoric of forced prostitution and their need for rehabilitation, the hostesses consider hostessing an expedient route to achieving a certain degree of social mobility and detest the violent working environment induced by the state policy.

From this ethnographic research, I argue that the intensive anti-trafficking and anti-prostitution campaigns deprives the hostesses of their rights, and patronizes them as victims. I argue that the state's focus on forced prostitution ignores the larger context within which force is used. That is, the global inequities of capital and labor that robs women of viable options and forces them into sweatshop labor or lucrative sex work. The state's moralistic campaigns against sex trafficking are intended to eradicate all forms of sex work and construe sex workers as sexual victims. Issues such as poverty, hunger, and low wages are disregarded in the trafficking discourse. Indeed, across the globe, sex workers' rights movements vehemently challenge the victim script in the trafficking discourse.

References

Gu, Qiuping. 2000. *Guoji Mingcheng Li Wo Men Hai You Duo Yuan* (Towards a Famous City in the World). *Dalian Ribao (Dalian Daily)*. May 25: C1.

Hershatter, Gail. 1997. *Dangerous Pleasures: Prostitution and Modernity in Twentieth-Century Shanghai*. Berkeley: University of California Press.

Jeffreys, Elaine. 2004. *China, Sex and Prostitution*. RouledgeCurzon.

Jian, Ping. 2001. *Caifang Shouji: Jingyan Dalian* (Interview Memoirs in Dalian). *Xinzhoukan (New Weekly)*. 10: 44.

Khan, Azizur Rahman and Carl Riskin. 1998. Income and Inequality in China: Composition, Distribution and Growth of Household Income, 1988-1995. *China Quarterly*. 154. June: 221-53.

Pan, Suiming. 1999. *Cun Zai Yu Hunag Niu: Zhong Guo Di Xia Xing Chan Ye Kao Cha* (*Existence and Irony: A Scrutiny of Chinese Underground Sex Industry*). Beijing: Qunyan Chubanshe (Qunyan Publishing House).

"*Sanpei xiaojie de Falu Baohu Wenti*" (Legal Protection of Hostesses). *Shenzhen Fazhi bao* (Shenzhen Law Newspaper). June 25. (2002)

Sun, Shaoguang. *Dalian E Mo Ba Xiaojie Fenshi Shiyi Kuai* (A Man in Dalian Divided a Hostess' Dead Body into Eleven Pieces). *Dongbei Xinwen Wang* (Northeastern News Net). December 12. (2003).

Zhang, Haibing. 2001. *Xinjiapo Yu Dalian (Singapore and Dalian)*.Shenyang: Liaoning Renmin Chubanshe (Liaoning People's Publishing House).

Notes

Chapter One

[1]   De Rode Draad (Red Thread), Stichting Tegen Vrouwenhandel (STV), and TAMPEP are NGOs with whom I have formed relations in the Netherlands.

[2]   The Coalition to Abolish Slavery and Trafficking (CAST) and the Young Women's Empowerment Project are organizations at which I have volunteered in the United States.

[3]   NGOs that fit within abolitionist frameworks include the Coalition Against Trafficking in Women (CATW), The Salvation Army, the European Women's Lobby, Equality Now, and Captive Daughters to name but a few. See Barry (1979) and Raymond and Hughes (2001).

[4]   The Global Alliance Against Trafficking in Women (GAATW) is well known for its critique of abolitionist perspectives that see all form of prostitution as exploitative. See Wijers and Lap-Chew (1997), Kempadoo and Doezema (1998), and Kampur (2003).

[5]   The International Organization of Migration situates trafficking in relation to movement but additionally focuses on human rights. The Coalition to Abolish Slavery and Trafficking similarly draws upon human rights perspectives.

[6]   The Network of Sex Work Projects and De Rode Draad propose that trafficking thrives as a result of criminalizing sex workers and their clients and they argue that decriminalizing and/or legalizing sex work can decrease incidents of trafficking since clients and sex workers are not discouraged from reporting exploitative labor practices to law enforcement.

[7]   See U.S. Department of State *Trafficking in Persons Report*, http://www.state.gov/g/tip/ rls/tiprpt/2006, and United Nations (2000) *The Protocol to Prevent, Suppress, and Punish Trafficking in Persons, Especially Women and Children, Supplementing the United Nations Convention Against Transnational Organized Crime*, http://www.odccp.org/crime_cicp_ signatures.html and Laczko (2002).

[8]   See Outshoorn (2005) and Jo Doezema (1998) for deconstructive analyses of the conflation between prostitution and trafficking.

[9]   See U.S. Department of State report, *The Link Between Prostitution and Trafficking*, (2004).

[10] NGOs based in the United States that advocate a pro-sex work/harms reductionist approach must look for nonfederal funding sources. For example, the Young Women's Empowerment Project, a harms-reductionist NGO based in Chicago works with young women that engage in commercial sex work. The YWEP does not attempt to "rehabilitate" the young women

nor do they force them to seek alternative work. Instead, the YWEP holds workshops and classes co-facilitated by the young women in an effort to share knowledge and build skills. As a consequence of its more progressive positionality, the YWEP has minimal funding; they currently receive money from the City of Chicago's Mayor's Office and private donors. For more information, see *http://www.youarepriceless.org*. For an interesting comparison, see *www.sageprojectinc.org*

[11] See Kathleen Barry (1979) and Donna Hughes (2000).

[12] Gail Kligman noted that arguments touting prostitution to be a "gateway" to trafficking resemble rhetorical claims in which marijuana is seen as a gateway drug to "harder" illegal substances like heroin.

[13] See Anne Gallagher (2001), Alexis Aronowitz (2001), and Kyle and Dale (2001).

[14] As a result of the passage of the 2000 TVPA, the U.S. Department of Health and Human Services was named the agency responsible for providing trafficked women, men and children with services and benefits. In order to receive DHHS certification, however, trafficked persons must have the support of the law enforcement officers that identified them. This speaks to my earlier point regarding the ways in which law enforcement and NGO biases may prevent *actual* trafficked persons from being identified as such. For more information on DHHS's Rescue and Restore Program, see: *http://www.acf.hhs.gov/trafficking/index.html*

[15] In August 2005, federal ICE agents "busted" an Asian spa in Dallas. ICE agent Coonen said this of the Korean women he interviewed: "The single biggest reason in this particular case is, I think, because the lion's share of the girls had the ability to move from one facility to another . . . they were not completely restricted. Many of them . . . knew that they voluntarily came to engage in this business with at least a bit of an understanding of the circumstances that you'll find when you get here" (Meyer, 2006).

[16] For a useful discussion of the challenges to conducting research on trafficking, see Kligman and Limoncelli (2005), Kelly (2005) and Tyldum and Brunovksis (2005).

[17] In July 1999, a court awarded $4 million to the Thai El Monte workers. For more information, see Sweatshop Watch. Available at: *http://www.sweatshopwatch.org/newsletters*.

[18] For more information about UCLA sponsored community partnerships, see *http://la.ucla.edu/Master.cfm?Page=Directory.cfm*.

Chapter Two

[1] The political stance of the current administration in the U.S. that is implied here, equally extends over to the ideological rhetoric adopted by the right-wing extremists in the Islamic Republic of Iran, emphasizing a sanction of *belonging to the self* (khody), as in being an insider, in contrast to standing on the exterior of the politically legitimate space, of belonging to *the other* (gheir-e khody).

[2] For example, in the aftermath of the Bam earthquake in 2003, volunteers and official border patrol discovered several trucks, loaded with orphaned children. Later reports determined that the children were abducted to be sold off abroad. (Ghanbarpour. 2003)

3   With an emphasis on the suffix of "ak" which implies smallness in both the size and age of the person.

4   The Prophet Mohammad freed up a black slave named Belal Habashi in a politically significant moment of Islamic history. Muslim communities in Iran—in formal religious teachings (sermons) as well as street plays (ta'ziye)—often pride themselves in the Prophet's attitude towards humanity and freedom.

5   See analysis offered by Paul Farmer (2001) and Mark Hunter (2002) based on their research on AIDS and HIV-prevention programs and public health models in Africa.

Chapter Three

1   For definition see UN Protocol to Prevent, Suppress and Punish Trafficking in Persons Definition of Trafficking in Persons, 2000.

2   LOKK (2003). (Landsorganisation af Kvindekrisecentre—National Association of Women's Crisis Centers) in the report *"Når drømme og håb forvandles til mareridt: Danske mænds vold mod udenlandske kvinder og børn"* ("When dreams and hopes turn into a nightmare: The violence of Danish men against women and children from other countries"). The report describes the shortcomings of knowledge about why women chose to "burn all their bridges."(p. 20).

3   All informants have been assigned fictive names.

4   There are 218 Thai citizens in Viborg county (Viborg Amt p. 10).

5   Pattaya is the center of the Thai tourist industry and, to a large extent, the country's sex industry.

6   Parallel to the "brain drain" from the poor countries of the world, but instead a "care drain."

7   Visit for example http://www.trafficked-women.org/trafficked.html (2004). CATW (Coalition against Trafficking in Women International) http://www.catwinternational.org/philos.htm or see Moustgaard & Brun (2001). Some groups are aware of the problem with a precise definition of trafficking. Se, for example, "UN Trafficking Protocol: Lost Opportunity to Protect the rights of Trafficked Persons" (2004) http://www.stop-traffic.org.news.html (As cited in Constable p. 23)

Chapter Four

1   The full name of this international protocol is the "Protocol to Prevent, Suppress and Punish Trafficking in Persons, especially Women and Children, Supplementing the United Nations Convention against Transnational Organized Crime."

2   In this paper, I use "Hong Kong" as the abbreviated version of the Hong Kong Special Administrative Region of China.

3   The study was conducted from September to November 2003. For full details on the methodology, see Briones (2006).

4   In this regard, I could have chosen any two similarly contrasting destinations such as Germany and Canada, respectively, New York and Riyadh, respectively and so on. For purposes of

research feasibility, Paris and Hong Kong seemed to me to be two sites in which I could undertake my research relatively quickly, safely (e.g., I would not have felt safe in Riyadh) and comprehensively. In addition, little was written about the situations of FODWs in Paris in contrast to the wide media coverage of migrant domestic workers' 'slavery' there. I thought that Paris (and because I also had sufficient French language skills) would provide the required stark contrast from the abundantly written situation of documented FODWs in Hong Kong.

5   While I was not able to speak with those who experienced the worst forms of slavery, which usually entail house imprisonment, contact with those recovering in a shelter enabled insights into these conditions. For example, I met Lani, who was living in a shelter in Paris, two weeks after an NGO had rescued her. Notably, Lani and the other respondents who 'reclassifed' their situations from slave to wageworker (Table 1) enabled further insight into the dynamics of FODW agency. The FODW names used here are pseudonyms.

6   Due to the undocumented status of FODWs in France, the figures given here are questionable. For instance, despite a 5-year lag, O'Dy (2001) uses the same estimate of 17000 as used by Anderson and Torrés in 1996. In contrast, personal communication with Ms Estrada of the Philippine Consulate in France (23 Sep 2003) suggested the estimate of the Filipino population to number at around 50 000 in France, with 20 000 located in Paris, and of which the great majority were women.

7   'Hong Kong citizenship' does not technically exist, but 'permanent residency' is its legal and practical equivalent. I retain the term 'citizenship' here for consistency in style. See here also Bell and Piper (2005, p. 199).

8   Also known as the New Conditions of Stay (NCS).

9   The Sino-British Joint Declaration on the Question of Hong Kong and the Basic Law provide the Hong Kong Special Administrative Region with full authority on its own matters of immigration control. It is in this respect that I refer to Hong Kong as a 'state' in this paper.

10   For further context to this question, see Momsen (1999) from which I borrow the terms "victim or victor."

11   This is perhaps best exemplified by those who classified their situations as "Former Slaves now Wageworkers." Although these respondents had experienced harrowing treatment in their previous work, they persisted (some even risked their lives escaping their abusive employers) with overseas domestic work, eventually finding fair employers. For their respective stories, see Briones, 2006, pp. 188-98.

12   The Visayas is an island/cultural group of the Philippines located in between the island groups of Luzon to the North and Mindanao to the South.

13   Aide Médicale d'Etat is a health service in France for foreigners, including those who are undocumented. This is a medical insurance provided by the state for access to medical care including examinations and prescriptions. Access for those who have lived in France for fewer than three years is limited to hospital care.

14   Virgo, the only respondent who deemed her income sufficient to live comfortably in the Philippines, and whose primary reason for migrating was to leave her husband (divorce is socially, religiously and legally unacceptable in the Philippines), nevertheless acknowledged that her "case would be in the great minority."

[15] The term "direct hire" has a double connotation in the recruitment business in Hong Kong. The first is used more commonly among recruitment agencies and refers to recruitment agency-facilitated hiring of workers directly from the Philippines. The second refers to the hiring by employers of interested Filipinas still in the Philippines, usually referred through familial/social networks. This second connotation is also the case for those going to Paris and other destinations without official bi-lateral labor program agreements with the Philippines.

[16] Mila, who has experienced both forms, tells how tighter immigration controls in France leave smuggling/trafficking as the only current option for entry: "The first time [1984] I came as a tourist...—just packed my bags with my visa. The second time..., it was more difficult so I had to come the clandestine way. It took me four months to reach France."

[17] For a full treatment of this approach, see Nussbaum (1988; 1992; 1995; 1998; 2000; 2003; 2004; 2006).

[18] For a full theorization, see Briones (2006).

Chapter Five

[1] This paper has been published in *Working in China: Ethnographies of Labor and Workplace Transformation*, ed. Ching Kwan Lee. Routledge. 2007.

[2] Gu 2000; Zhang 2001.

[3] This is the official figure of the city's population (in the four central districts).

[4] Zhang. (2001) 142. Municipal officials interviewed estimated a floating population in Dalian of one million people, from all over China.

[5] *News Weekly,* 2001.

[6] Jian 2001; Khan 1998: 44.

[7] Interview conducted in 2001.

[8] See Hershatter 1997.

[9] Although karaoke bars are legal, they have always been one of the government's main "culture purging" targets. It is claimed that they work against the state's cultural logic in three aspects: (1) Socialist business should prioritize the needs of people and serve the people. It should be different from the commercial system, where the pure objective is to pursue and procure sudden huge profit. Many bar bosses operate their business by cheating customers and providing erotic services. (2) "Erotic company" (*seqing peishi*) is illegal and immoral and runs counter to socialist "spiritual civilization." Such "ugly phenomena" associated with capitalism should be wiped out to maintain the healthy and inspiring socialist cultural environment and "civilized consumption." (3) Juxtaposed against socialist recreations enjoyed by the masses, karaoke bars are more individually based, places where individuals pursue and express their "repulsive and hideous" desires to show off their performing talents and satisfy their sexual demands. In view of these reasons, karaoke bars regularly undergo a purging process to become part of "spiritual civilization." Frequent police raids are part of this process.

[10] Male dominance of the business world in China is reinforced by the use of karaoke bars to entertain clients. While I heard that occasionally female businesswomen entertained male clients, I never witnessed such an arrangement myself.

[11] See Pan 1999: 13-14.

[12] Reconstructing the history of karaoke bars in Dalian proved to be exceedingly difficult. A combination of official denial and embarrassment has ensured that no publicly open records were kept on the subject, and the same attitude undoubtedly dissuaded any interested parties from prying. To piece together the story, I was therefore forced to rely entirely on the oral accounts of government officials in different divisions of the municipal Bureau of Culture.

[13] See Jeffreys, 2004.

[14] This policy is designed to boost the bar owners' sense of pride as contributors to the socialist culture market. Inculcated with this new thought, bar owners will take the initiative to transform their bars into civilized spaces, where clients' lofty sentiments can be nurtured.

[15] This is in the upscale karaoke bar where hostesses were not living in the bar. I lived with the hostesses in the low-tier karaoke bar in the red-light district.

[16] After I received a visa to the United States, the government withdrew my ID card. The only ID left me is my passport. A passport without an ID card indicates that the person in question does not reside in China.

[17] This information is taken from my interview with the political officials in the municipal government.

[18] "*Sanpei xiaojie de Falu Baohu Wenti*" (Legal Protection of Hostesses). *Shenzhen Fazhi bao* (*Shenzhen Law Newspaper*). 25 June 25 2002.

[19] Sun, Shaoguang. "*Dalian E Mo Ba Xiaojie Fenshi Shiyi Kuai*" (A Man in Dalian Divided a Hostess' Dead Body into Eleven Pieces). *Dongbei Xinwen Wang* (Northeastern News Net), 12 December 2003.

www.ingramcontent.com/pod-product-compliance
Lightning Source LLC
Chambersburg PA
CBHW031253280526
45784CB00004B/1836